The Political Interview

The Political Interview

Broadcast Talk in the Interactional Combat Zone

Ian Hutchby

LEXINGTON BOOKS
Lanham • Boulder • New York • London

Published by Lexington Books
An imprint of The Rowman & Littlefield Publishing Group, Inc.
4501 Forbes Boulevard, Suite 200, Lanham, Maryland 20706
www.rowman.com

86-90 Paul Street, London EC2A 4NE

Copyright © 2022 by The Rowman & Littlefield Publishing Group, Inc.

All rights reserved. No part of this book may be reproduced in any form or by any electronic or mechanical means, including information storage and retrieval systems, without written permission from the publisher, except by a reviewer who may quote passages in a review.

British Library Cataloguing in Publication Information Available

Library of Congress Cataloging-in-Publication Data

Names: Hutchby, Ian, author.
Title: The political interview : broadcast talk in the interactional combat zone / Ian Hutchby.
Description: Lanham : Lexington Books, [2022] | Includes bibliographical references and index.
Identifiers: LCCN 2021032452 (print) | LCCN 2021032453 (ebook) | ISBN 9781793640093 (cloth) | 9781793640116 (paperback) | ISBN 9781793640109 (ebook)
Subjects: LCSH: Interviewing in journalism. | Broadcast journalism—Political aspects. | Discourse analysis—Political aspects. | Mass media—Political aspects. | Interviewing in mass media. | Communication in politics.
Classification: LCC PN4784.I6 H88 2021 (print) | LCC PN4784.I6 (ebook) | DDC 070.4/3—dc23
LC record available at https://lccn.loc.gov/2021032452
LC ebook record available at https://lccn.loc.gov/2021032453

Contents

Acknowledgements		vii
1	The Political News Interview in Context	1
2	Analyzing Interviews as Arenas of Language Use	17
3	Total Mediatization: A Media Ecology of the Broadcast Political Interview	31
4	Rules of Engagement: The Conventional Political Interview	51
5	"It's a Simple Question": The Adversarial Political Interview	73
6	"So My Position Is . . . ": Explanatory Answers and Agenda Contests	97
7	Opinion, Emotion, and Personalization in the Hybrid Political Interview	115
8	Tribuneship, Objectivity, and the Public Interest	141
9	The Political Interview in an Opinionated World: Some Concluding Reflections	159
Appendix: Glossary of Transcription Symbols		169
References		173
Index		183
About the Author		187

Acknowledgements

I am grateful to the copyright holders for permission to reproduce the following materials:

Chapter 3 originally appeared as Hutchby, I. (2016) "Infelicitous talk: Politicians' words and the media ecology in three British political gaffes." *Journal of Language and Politics*, Vol. 15, No.6: 667-687. Copyright © 2016 by John Benjamins Publishing Company. DOI: 10.1075/jlp.15.6.01hut

Chapter 6 originally appeared in a slightly different form as Hutchby, I. (2020) "'So my position is': So-prefaced answers and epistemic authority in British news interviews." *Journal of Language and Politics*, Vol. 19, No. 4: 563-582. Copyright © 2021 by John Benjamins Publishing Company. DOI: 10.1075/jlp.19089.hut

Parts of chapter 7 originally appeared in Hutchby, I. (2011) "Non-neutrality and argument in the Hybrid Political Interview." *Discourse Studies*, Vol. 13, No. 3: 349-366. Copyright © 2011 by SAGE Publications. DOI: 10.1177/1461445611400665

Chapter One

The Political News Interview in Context

The landscape of broadcast news media is constantly changing, partly under the influence of changing technology, but also due to changes in approaches to the social role of television journalism. This book takes a sociological and linguistic approach to examining some of these changes, focusing on one particular domain of broadcasting: the political news interview. Training its analytical lens on the fine-grained details of live broadcast news interview discourse, the book looks at a range of contemporary developments in the ways that interviews with politicians, and also other political actors—commentators, experts, think-tank representatives, policy advisors, bloggers, and so on—are conducted. It examines some of the broader social dimensions and consequences of changing styles of interviewing; in particular, approaches to journalistic neutralism, adversarialism and tribuneship in different broadcast interview formats, by focusing on the discourse practices associated with them. In the process, the book draws into question not just the evasion and slipperiness of politicians in the present era of what some journalists are calling "post-truth"; but also the ethics and neutrality of journalists in an increasingly hybrid environment where probing can readily morph into position taking, and the discursive boundaries of "interview" can sometimes blur into "argument."

THE RELEVANCE OF THE LIVE NEWS INTERVIEW

Even in the era of internet news, social media, blogging, podcasts and other forms of "citizen journalism," interviews with key political figures, or about major political issues, remain a staple of the most significant news broadcasts in all the major economic regions of the world. The live broadcast interview is one of the key ways in which political news and opinions are conveyed to, and interpreted for, the public. Major broadcasters in the UK, US and elsewhere around the world run 24-hour news channels whose output is liberally peppered with interviews, amid the other main news vehicles: narration read direct to camera by an anchor, affiliative interviews (Montgomery, 2007) between special correspondents and anchors, or field reports wired in by outside correspondents.

On occasion, a particular political interview can become newsworthy in its own right. This can happen when a journalist grills an evasive politician in a notably effective way; or when an interview is otherwise held to have been a journalistic coup. Conversely, a single interview can become newsworthy if, for example, an interviewee stages a walk-out in the course of a live broadcast. Such events are comparatively rare, and it is their rarity that draws them to the forefront of the public consciousness. More common, more prosaic, though in many ways no less consequential, are the sorts of political gaffes (unintentional or ill-advised remarks resulting in embarrassment, controversy and sometimes resignation) that can result from conduct in political news interviews.

Media interviews are also significant in terms of the role they can play in the unfolding of political stories within the temporal structure of the news cycle (Golding and Elliott, 1979; Schlesinger, 1978). The news cycle itself is an evolving process, as the internet and social networking increasingly merge with the traditional outlets of the press and broadcasting into a "hybrid media system" (Chadwick, 2014). But broadcast interviews retain significant power in the development of news stories even within this changing media ecology. When a major story breaks, even if the origins of it are based in the new media rather than the "old" media of broadcasting or the press, it remains the case that leading political actors will rapidly be sought out for interview appearances in newspapers, on radio and on television in order to put forward a response to events.

Perhaps most significantly, throughout this book I will argue that the broadcast political interview, in the contemporary environment of what I will call *total mediatization*, can be seen as an interactional combat zone. It is an arena of language use in which, within the potentially sterile environment of question-answer exchanges, journalists and political actors engage in thinly veiled contestation over the representation of current political ideas, policies, strategies and agendas. Some years ago, Clayman and Heritage (2002: 25) referred to the news interview as a "game" whose "participants are locked in competition, and with varying levels of skill . . . deploy their moves strategically in pursuit of divergent goals and objectives." Yet as they go on to say, it is more than just a game because, in the end, "there may be ramifications for personal careers, for public affairs, and sometimes for the march of history."

This book will also develop the idea that what we think of as "the broadcast political interview" is, in the current environment, not one single type of thing. Although there are distinctive norms and conventions of speaking that are constitutive of "an interview" as compared, say, to "a conversation," the media phenomenon that we may understand commonsensically as a political interview does not appear in only one conventional shape.

The basic argument of the book is this: over the last two to three decades, as news interview outlets have proliferated and news interviewer conduct has evolved, a situation has emerged in which the political interview itself is a hybrid media phenomenon; a form of institutional interaction that embraces a range of different formats that in turn embody, in the very structural organization of their discourse practices, different journalistic conceptions of the relationship between questions and answers, truth, objectivity, and the representation of the public interest.

In earlier accounts, based largely on the analysis of twentieth-century political interviewing, the argument was that this evolution in practices saw a shift mainly from more deferential to more adversarial interviewing techniques; the role of the interviewer shifting from neutral questioner to active investigator (for example, Schudson, 1994; Clayman and Heritage, 2002). While acknowledging this particular history in its own terms, and drawing on more recent research into news interview conduct (for example, Ekström and Patrona, 2011; Ekström and Tolson, 2013; Mast et al., 2017; Montgomery, 2007; Thornborrow and Montgomery, 2010), the present analysis suggests that for the twenty-first century political interview, the key evolutionary shift is one from neutralism to non-neutralism; from interview to argument: and the role of the interviewer from investigator to inquisitor, tribune of the people, or even socio-political advocate.

AUTHENTIC TALK AND THE INTERVIEW SOCIETY

Against this background, it is useful to consider a popular sociological conception of interviews as a particularly "authentic" form of interaction in the ways they offer insight not just into social processes, but individual motives and beliefs (Atkinson and Silverman, 1997; Silverman, 2017). In the social sciences, the idea of interviews as eliciting supposedly authentic or subjectively genuine discourse goes back at least to the idea of "thick description" in ethnographic anthropology (Ryle, 1949; Geertz, 1973) and the influential Chicago School of sociology (Blumer, 1969). In popular culture, also, it has been central to long-standing media genres such as the celebrity talk show (Atkinson and Silverman, 1997; Tolson, 2006), the radio phone-in (Hutchby,

1996, 2001a) and confessional or confrontational reality shows such as *Ricki Lake*, *Jerry Springer*, *Oprah* or *Jeremy Kyle* (Carbaugh, 1988; Tolson, 2001; Thornborrow, 2014), as well as early morning and early evening magazine shows, current affairs and documentary programs.

The idea that we therefore live in an "interview society" (Silverman, 2017) where we treat the interview as having the potential, at least, to reveal something authentic about its subject was neatly reflected in the following comments, from a 2015 article in the *Guardian* newspaper about the interview style of then newly-installed British Labour Party leader Jeremy Corbyn: "[Corbyn] has not been media-trained and a colleague of his says, 'The thing about him is that he is just authentic. It's effective because people can see it's genuine . . . he just answers the question. I think the broadcasters have been kind of unhinged by it'." Another journalist quoted in the same article suggests that "such authenticity is at a 'premium' in the modern age when many viewers do not trust politicians," pointing out that "Corbyn has frequently admitted he does not know the answers to some questions" (Conlan, 2015). There is a tendency, therefore, to value straight speaking as *authentic* by both journalists and audiences, even if such authenticity is recognized mainly by its rarity.

One place where we can see this valorization of authenticity in journalism is in the long-form, set-piece, or as I will call it, the "spotlight" political interview. A general distinction can be made, in the contemporary environment of broadcast political interviewing, between two main categories of interview. The first is what I will call the "workaday" interview that occurs within the ordinary running order of daily news broadcasts. Such interviews can run from as little as half a minute up to perhaps five minutes in length. They are by far the most commonplace interview types encountered on radio and television, and their interactional structures are considered at greater length in chapter 4. The second type is the spotlight interview, designed to delve in depth into the political positions and motivations of individual high-profile political actors. These interviews can have a running time anywhere from ten or twenty minutes to an hour; and in exceptional cases, even longer.

Workaday and spotlight interviews have very different functions, as well as different scheduling positions, within the overall political media environment. Spotlight political interviews, which occupy their own slot in the news schedule and in which the politician is subjected to a long and detailed set of questions across a range of topics, are sometimes high-profile media events in their own right, as when they involve incumbent prime ministers or presidents, or leaders challenging for such roles. Sometimes they become high profile due to the nature of the discussion that transpired during the extended slot.

For decades, there have existed political news programs that are heavily or exclusively based on the production of spotlight interviews as their main fare. In the US the format was pioneered by programs such as *The News-Hour*, *NightLine* and *Meet the Press* (Clayman and Heritage, 2002). In the UK, at the time of writing, there are at least six or seven regular, nightly or weekly broadcasts that feature long-form interviews, including *The Andrew Marr Show*, *Politics Live*, *Newsnight*, *Today*, *Peston*, and *Channel 4 News*. The BBC's *HARDtalk* is a particularly clear example: eschewing any more general news coverage, its format specializes in single issue installments in which the host subjects a selected political actor to thirty minutes of "hard" questioning on an issue of the day.

Historically speaking, perhaps the most high-profile and oft-cited spotlight political interview was that conducted in 1977 by British broadcaster David Frost with Richard Nixon, following his resignation in the wake of the Watergate scandal. Recorded over a period of four weeks, it was broadcast in a series of installments during which Frost probed Nixon on a range of controversial topics associated with Watergate and its aftermath. The interview was ultimately considered dramatic enough to be turned into a Broadway play and subsequently a Hollywood film (*Frost/Nixon*, Universal, 2008).

This historic broadcast exemplifies an idealization of the political interview as media event, in which the point is to provide a detailed delving into the realm of the personal viewpoints and embodied responses of elite public figures; ideally bringing into public view their authentic, private selves rather than their professionally performed political personae.

Frost had for many years hosted his own interview show on British television, *The Frost Programme*, and had developed an interviewing style that was highly detailed, intelligent and often controversial. For example, his 1967 spotlight interview with Dr. Emil Savundra, a business tycoon accused of defrauding the policy claimants of an insurance company he had set up and then liquidated, was conducted in front of an audience consisting mainly of those very policy claimants. Even though Savundra was subsequently convicted, the interview's adversarial nature led to it being described critically by the judge in the case, in what appears to be the first appearance of this phrase, as a "trial by television." The interview with Nixon was recorded when Frost was still at the peak of his form; and his questioning led the president, even in the face of his own great caution, to reveal many significant insights into his beliefs and motives regarding Watergate, the processes of government, and other matters.

In recent years, the broadcasting of specialized, extended interviews with high-profile politicians has come to be a standard feature of news broadcasting especially around election times. Flagship evening news programs in

Britain, the United States and many European countries set aside lengthy slots in which the leaders, and sometimes deputy leaders or running mates, of the major political parties are subjected to detailed interviews on their proposed policies for leading the nation. These are in addition to the leaders' debates which, originating in the US but increasingly being used in Britain and other countries (Coleman, 2010), show party leaders sharing a platform to discuss and debate policy issues in front of a live studio audience, with a journalist acting as moderator.

Spotlight interviews are therefore significant in many ways; but in the day-to-day unfolding of the 24-hour rolling news schedules of modern broadcasting, the workaday political interview dominates, and is a very different journalistic beast. Within the schedule of a daily news broadcast, the time available to engage in detailed probing around specific points or attempting to reveal the authentic political self of the interviewee is severely limited. In these more routine interviews, the interviewer's task is as much about trying to keep the interviewee's talk constrained on-topic within the short available time slot (Clayman, 1989), as he or she engages in the mundane work of managing the everyday delivery of political information in what I describe, below, as the contemporary cultural conditions of "total mediatization."

Writing about the relationship between the interview and authenticity, Atkinson and Silverman (1997: 322) concluded that the interview does not produce "any more authentic or pure a reflection of the self than any other socially organized set of practices"; instead our analytic gaze should focus on the practices by which the interview seeks to *construct* a sense of authentic self, rather than to reflect one. In a similar vein, in subsequent chapters, I look at the various types of interview in broadcast political news in terms of their socially organized sets of practices, their construction of more or less contentious discourses around contemporary political issues, rather than their reflection of, or failure to reflect, authentic political subjectivities.

TOTAL MEDIATIZATION

The political interview also remains key to our understanding of broader issues, such as the relationship between the media, public opinion, and public knowledge. In the sphere of public information and representation, broadcast interviews have for a long time been identified as crucial arenas in which one of the key social processes of modern times—the "mediatization" of politics and political issues—has taken place:

> Much of contemporary political discourse is mediatized political discourse. Its major genres are no longer just the traditional genres of politics, they are also

genres of the media. Traditional political activities and their genres—parliamentary debates, party conferences, international conferences—carry on, but they too are represented in the media. ... At the same time, genres for political discourse that the media themselves generate are increasingly important for politicians—most notably the political interview, but also, for instance, phone-in programs. (Fairclough, 1995: 188)

In fact, the mediatization of politics is a process that has been underway since the advent of serious investigative journalism in the newspaper reporting of the early twentieth century, when journalists began to see themselves less as the chroniclers of social and political events and more as inquirers on behalf of the public interest. Media historians such as Schudson (1994) and Scannell and Cardiff (1991) have traced these developments. At first it was a slow process, in which it sometimes seemed, in Britain especially, as if the politicians had the upper hand.

For instance, in the 1920s the fledgling British Broadcasting Company, eager to widen its influence as a bringer of news and entertainment to the public, entered an agreement with the government (known as the Charter) to become the recognized national broadcasting company (the British Broadcasting Corporation or BBC) with an effective monopoly funded by a license fee payable under law by anyone who owned a radio or, later, television set. While the license policy is still in operation today, the terms of the original Charter were highly restrictive, especially in regard to the ability of the BBC to report on "controversial matters" in the news (Scannell and Cardiff, 1991). The established interests of the newspapers and the press owners played a significant part, along with the politicians, in constraining the BBC's remit; and indeed the constraints placed by the government upon the early BBC were far more onerous than in other countries at the time, either in Europe or, especially, the USA, where broadcasting licenses were granted not by the government but by the independent Federal Communications Commission. This fact was used by the BBC's influential founding chief, John Reith, in his eventually successful attempts to have the reporting constraints lifted, albeit with an injunction, still in place today, that the BBC reports political matters with "due impartiality."

In more recent years, especially with the advent of 24-hour rolling news coverage and the increasing proliferation and influence of satellite and cable news channels, the process of mediatization has gradually accelerated to the stage of what we might now call *total mediatization*. Total mediatization refers to the sense in which contemporary political action is enveloped by media scrutiny; as well as the way in which the technological forms of mediation are diversified rather than concentrated.

Total mediatization is similar in some respects to what Strömbäck (2008) has termed the "fourth phase" in the mediatization of politics. For Strömbäck, mediatization should be understood as a process characterized by the changing relations of autonomy and dependence associated with the different "logics" of politics, on the one hand, and media on the other. Media logic, for Strömbäck, means the news values and storytelling techniques that broadcasting and the press make use of to attract audiences (see also Bell, 1991). By political logic, Strömbäck means the processes of decision-making and policy implementation, as well as the distribution of political power, such as the formation of government cabinets, and the constitution of political elites through elections. The four phases of mediatization he traces out reveal how the latter becomes increasingly dominated by the former, such that in the fourth phase, the media logic becomes more important in defining not just the significance, but the actuality of events than the logic of political systems or individual agents such as politicians, press officers and so on. Strömbäck (2008: 240) argues that while mediatization in this sense can be "managed" by political actors, it is "a problem that requires constant attention."

It is this requirement for constant attention that leads me to prefer the term total mediatization to refer to the present media/politics conjuncture, at least when considering politics at the national and international level. The broadcast interview is one form of political discourse that plays a key role here. The reason for this is that interviews are not stand-alone events taking place in a discursive vacuum. As we see in more detail in chapter 3, the broadcast interview plays a part in a much wider ecology of mediatized political discourses to which it is reflexively related.

This combination of the increasing power over current affairs of media logic, coupled with the widening ecology of communication in which political action is situated, may ultimately be responsible for the perception, among certain commentators, that politicians and their communications managers are trying to fight back against the media by effectively ignoring its agenda-setting.

EVOLUTION OF MEDIA INTERVIEW FORMATS

If mediatization is an evolving and hybridizing process, the same can be said about the media interview itself. Schudson (1994) traced the early stages of the news interview's evolution by examining the shift from early forms of interview, in which the journalist mainly adopted the deferential role of stenographer or chronicler, to news interviews in which journalists took on a far more analytical and investigative role. This shift, according to Schudson, began to take place in the printed press in the late nineteenth century. Throughout the twentieth century, and especially with the advent of mass access to television broadcasting, trends toward greater adversarialism have been seen as a further development of the journalist's investigative role (Clayman and Heritage, 2002). Moving into the twenty-first century, we witness the development of television news programs that drive this evolution further by developing more personalized forms of news interviewing, hybridizing the very forms of talk and interaction in which the interview takes place, and in some cases foregrounding the journalist as "advocate," "inquisitor" or "arbiter of truth" (Ekström, Kroon and Nylund, 2006; Ekström and Patrona, 2011; Thornborrow and Montgomery, 2010, Mast, Coesemans and Temmerman, 2017).

To some extent, these later developments are linked in with the confluence of digitization and deregulation in broadcasting policy that has led to a proliferation of news channels running twenty-four hours a day, seven days a week, and serving niche as well as generic public interests (Silvia, 2001). The resultant global news culture has been analyzed in terms of wider trends in which broadcasting is critiqued for its increasing marketization, and the shaping of its output by commercial and corporate agendas into the hybrid forms of "infotainment" (Thussu, 2008). Many of the journalistic practices of cable and satellite news are less constrained by the commitment to impartiality and objectivity that is often written into the licensing agreements of public service-oriented news channels. For some analysts, the blending of information and entertainment in the former context is simultaneously aligned with the influence of business interests and, specifically, the promulgation of conservative or populist ideas. For example, "[for cable channel Fox News] a preference for neo-conservative opinions over news should be recognized as a matter of corporate policy" (Meehan, 2005:2).

In this kind of critical political economy approach, the trend toward infotainment and other hybrid genres impacts fundamentally not just on the nature of political journalism, but also on the role of the media in the democratic process. And without doubt this is an important issue. But my starting point in this book is that rather than treating the political economy *underpinning* the discourse as the preeminent focus, we need to address the complex details of *how* political alignments and disputes are managed in actual, real-time mediated discourse.

One way of doing this might be to take particular news stories and examine closely their unfolding over time, within and across the range of media involved in their production, using a form of real-time ethnographic (or "mediagraphic") observation (for an example of this, see Chadwick, 2011).

Another approach—the one adopted in the present book—is to focus the analytical lens on the fine details of the language and interactional structures of broadcast interviews themselves. Interviews are, primarily, occasions of talk: talk in interaction between professional journalists and political actors of various sorts. In order to understand the ways that the media interview as a discourse form is developing and changing, we have to begin with detailed empirical investigation of the constitutive interactional and functional structures of the discourse itself, produced in real time by interviewers and interviewees. Studies using the methods of conversation analysis (Hutchby and Wooffitt, 2008) have begun from such a position, succinctly put by Heritage, Clayman and Zimmerman (1988: 80): "Although the medium may not be the message, the interactional structures through which broadcast news is conveyed must necessarily contribute to the content and appearance of news messages."

This methodological approach, outlined in more detail in chapter 2, is part of a broader trend in recent media research known variously as "media discourse," "broadcast talk" or "media talk" studies (Hutchby, 2006). This focuses on the discourse practices of broadcasters and the public within media environments in order to explore the ways that modern broadcasting engages with public issues and the concerns of ordinary civil society. News interviews and political debates have been analyzed as involving formal turn-taking systems in which journalists adopt professional norms of neutrality, while politicians and other public figures use careful or highly circumspect means of taking up—or avoiding taking up—positions on topics of key public interest. Participants nevertheless orient to a turn-taking format which centrally involves chains of question-answer-next question sequences (Greatbatch, 1988). This is, of course, very different from turn-taking in mundane conversation, where roles are not restricted to those of questioner and answerer, and where the type and order of turns in a given interaction may freely vary. During the course of an interview, normative rules operate, which means that attempts to move outside the boundaries of the question-answer framework may be subject to sanction (Clayman and Heritage, 2002).

Beginning from this standpoint, a wide variety of aspects of news interview conduct have been investigated over many years of research. These range from the basic ways in which the turn-taking format is managed (Greatbatch, 1988) to the means by which interviewees seek to shift the agendas pursued in interviewers' questions (Greatbatch, 1986); from the ways in which interviewers display their journalistic objectivity in questions (Clayman, 1988, 1992) to the means by which debate and disagreement are managed in the context of different interview formats (Clayman and Heritage, 2002; Emmertsen, 2007; Greatbatch, 1992; Rendle-Short, 2007; Roca-Cuberes, 2013; Romaniuk, 2013).

A further range of studies have argued that we should view news interviewing through a wider lens than the question-answer turn-taking system and the management of neutrality and interviewee challenges. For example, Thornborrow and Montgomery (2010) collected studies which explore the ways in which public and private boundaries are being blurred or broken down in contemporary news interviews. Others have focused on the international variability of interview practices, adversarial styles and challenges to interviewer neutralism in different political cultures (Ekström, Kroon and Nylund, 2006; Ekström and Patrona, 2011; Ekström and Tolson, 2013; Kantara, 2012).

In an influential study, Montgomery (2007) argues that the focus on *political* interviewing in most of this work is itself too restrictive and overshadows the extent to which news interviews are also about personal testimony, on-the-spot correspondence and eyewitness reports. In his view, the interview should be situated within its enveloping broadcast context, namely the range of discourses that constitute the whole phenomenon of "broadcast news." Within the framework of news production, news programs utilize a range of interview types that differ depending on whether the interviewer is in the studio or on location at the scene, or according to the categorial identity of the interviewee in relation to the event being reported upon.

He identifies four types of interview. The "expert" interview involves a professional journalist and a professional representative of some important body (the government, a business organization, the health service, and so on). The "experiential" interview involves a professional journalist and a lay person, such as an eyewitness at a newsworthy event. The "affiliated" interview involves two (or more) professional journalists: one in the studio, another at the scene of a newsworthy event. Here in particular the conventional question-answer structure can become more informal as the on-location journalist relays, often extempore, their interpretation of the latest events in live interaction with the studio anchor. Political interviews are gathered under Montgomery's fourth heading, the "accountability" interview. Here, the key interactional feature is that the interviewee (a politician) is being held to account for actions or statements which the interviewer treats as somehow controversial.

Montgomery makes a persuasive case. However, while I agree that the broadcast interview is not a straightforward or homogeneous phenomenon, the main aim of the present book is to highlight different aspects of that diversification. Primarily, as should be clear from the earlier discussion, I retain the focus on political interviewing; but I argue that this category itself needs to be understood in a more variegated way, taking in a broader range of interview types, along with a wider variety of broadcast outlets.

HYBRIDITY AND REFLEXIVITY IN NEWS INTERVIEW DISCOURSE

In the current environment of televised news, the political interview is not something that takes place solely within the "official" format of mainstream news broadcasting. Alongside the largely mainstream political interviews analyzed in earlier conversation analytic work, we now need to incorporate non-mainstream hybrid and reflexive forms in which challenges to the normative interview format and the premises of journalistic neutrality are being mounted in contemporary broadcasting (Mast, Coesemans and Temmerman, 2017).

For example, a range of work has focused on hybridizing phenomena such as infotainment and confrontainment: programs in which interview turn-taking systems are merged with the genres of comedy and satire, such as the long-running *Daily Show* on Comedy Central which ironically describes itself as a "fake news show" (Brants and Neijens, 1998; Luginbühl, 2007; Otto, Glogger and Boukes, 2016; Thussu, 2008); or chat show–based interviews hosted by celebrities in which ironic and playful forms of questioning are used to try and reveal "authentic" aspects of politicians' personae (Baym, 2013; Ekström, 2011; Loeb, 2017).

As this work suggests, hybrid news formats are not entirely new. Indeed, early on in their major work on the news interview, Clayman and Heritage (2002) make a passing observation on *Larry King Live*, a show that ran from 1985-2010 on cable news channel CNN. As they remark, that show was frequently concerned with politics, the host conducting interviews with political actors in the conventional question-answer format; yet it also incorporated features of talk radio (Hutchby, 1996), airing calls from the public. It was thus an "early hybrid of the news interview and talk radio genres" (Clayman and Heritage, 2002: 8; see also Lauerbach, 2004).

Around the turn of the century, hybrid formats for serious political news started to grow considerably in significance, especially on the US-based cable channels. At the height of its popularity, one of the original, and most influential, hybrid news shows on cable TV, Fox News' nightly *The O'Reilly Factor*, was regularly attracting audiences of up to 2 million (twice the nightly audience of *Larry King Live*, for example). Significant audiences were also being drawn by other leading cable news channels in the US such as MSNBC and CNN. It seems clear therefore that we need to incorporate these and other program formats into a more nuanced, as well as more global, definition of "the political interview" as a media discourse form.

The growing significance of hybrid news formats is bound up with a wider series of changes that, for a number of years now, have been taking place in the way that television news is presented. Many of these changes have been driven by the satellite broadcasters—especially the highly successful Sky News channel—and by other non-standard, subscription-based channels. These changes can be summarized in broad terms as follows:

a) Increasing use of multimodality, including satellite links, web-based resources, mobile communications technologies and the social media (Chadwick, 2014).
b) Increasing adversarialism on the part of interviewers—a next step in the general evolution of journalistic conduct described by Schudson (1994).
c) Increasing informalization of broadcast talk along the lines of "conversationalization" and "sociability" —further developments of processes first described by Scannell (1989, 1991) and Fairclough (1995).
d) An increase in hybrid news formats that position the journalist not just as investigator or reporter but as analyst and even, in certain news contexts, as opinion-giver or socio-political advocate—related to general processes of hybridization in news formats (Ekström and Patrona, 2011; Mast et al., 2017).
e) A resultant raft of challenges to the traditionally conceived "neutralistic" role of the broadcast news journalist (Clayman, 1988) that derived from the professional ethos of objective reporting (Montgomery, 2011).

In summary, as well as evolving through time, the political interview is diversifying in form. My aim in this book is to apply the fine-grained observational techniques associated with conversation analysis to examine a range of different types of political news interview, specifically incorporating those in which challenges to the normative interview format and the premises of journalistic neutralism are being mounted in contemporary broadcasting. I examine a range of these interview variations, or *modalities*, using empirical data consisting of live to air broadcast interviews from both historical and contemporary periods.

The "conventional political interview" (CPI) is a format in which both interviewer and interviewee comply in observing fairly strict conventions both on how to take turns at speaking, and on what topics can be discussed. This turn-taking structure is characterized by two main types of sequence that, as early work showed, are uniquely adapted to the professional journalistic constraints of neutralism: *question-answer-next question* (the avoidance of third-turn acknowledgement of interviewees' answers); and *question-answer-formulation* (use of third-turn summaries to suggest rewordings and sometimes challenges to interviewees' answers) (Clayman, 1992; Greatbatch, 1988; Heritage, 1985). This conventional interview type emerged in the early days of broadcasting (Schudson, 1994) but can still be found in many broadcast contexts today.

The "adversarial political interview" (API) is closely related to the CPI but involves more aggressive lines of questioning that often take the appearance of the forms of talk found in courtroom cross-examination. Indeed, Montgomery (2007: 206) points out that one of the earliest proponents of adversarial interviewing on British TV, Sir Robin Day, originally had a background as a courtroom advocate. Many leading British politicians also have training and sometimes practical experience as attorneys and can be adept at using similar methods in challenging or resisting the interviewer's line of questioning. The line between CPI and API modalities can sometimes be blurred: for instance, interviewers' use of "formulations" can be cooperative or adversarial; while many question formats in the API at least superficially retain the CPI's basic orientation to neutralism on the interviewer's part.

The "hybrid political interview" (HPI) is a more recent development that combines adversarial techniques with features of discourse genres from outside political news broadcasting—for example, talk radio and everyday argument. In this format, the question-answer structure of the CPI is retained to some extent, but the interviewer (and sometimes the interviewee as well) freely moves between that structure and forms of talk that are more closely associated with disputing and accusing than with interviewing (Hutchby, 2011a). The norms of journalistic neutralism that are central to the CPI and the API are more or less completely dispensed with in the HPI (Hutchby, 2011b). The question-answer sequence of the standard news interview may shift not just into assertoric forms of questioning, but into full-blown assertoric sequences: the exchange of assertion and counter-assertion that is one of the basic grounds of mundane argument (Coulter, 1990).

Other primary features of the HPI include the interviewer's greater license to *personalize* argumentative standpoints; to foreground his or her *agency* as a spokesperson "for" certain political stances or social forces; and, perhaps most noticeably, the license taken by the interviewer to "go ballistic" in emotionally heightened episodes of direct confrontation with the interviewee. All this in turn has implications for the relationship between broadcast journalism, politics, and the representation of public interest.

OUTLINE OF THE BOOK

Chapter 2 takes us into the empirical detail of the book by discussing its underpinning methodological approach. The chapter presents an introduction to the approach known as conversation analysis, outlining the background to this method, its approach to analyzing "naturally-occurring" data, and its application to the study of media discourse, and in particular, the news interview.

Chapter 3 goes on to provide a framework in which to think about the significance of "the interview" both in terms of recent sociological thinking, and the development of media in relation to political communication. It discusses further the idea of the *total mediatization* of political discourse and action, suggesting that the broadcast interview is a key location in which the effects of total mediatization play out in observable terms. While this theme continues to inform the analysis in the chapters that follow, an initial illustration of its significance is made by exploring a number of political "gaffes" that have unfolded at different points in the last twenty-five years, looking at how the mediatized configuration of such events has changed in that time.

Chapter 4 then provides an account of the main features of the conventional political interview format, or CPI. Drawing on a range of conversation analytic work conducted from the 1990s to the present day, it uses contemporary data to outline the main interactional features of the interview as a form of institutional interaction, introduces the concept of "neutralism" that is central to conventional interview journalism, and explores a range of ways that the resources of language and grammar can be used by journalists to engage in questioning that is both objective and challenging.

Chapters 5 through 8 draw upon a sample of contemporary interviews involving different journalists and politicians to analyze the structural features of interviewer and interviewee conduct as it occurs in what I describe as the "interactional combat zone" of more adversarial and aggressive interview types. The approach is broadly comparative. Having begun in chapter 4 with the conventional interview turn-taking system and the ways in which it is particularly adapted to the constraints of neutralistic reporting of news, I move on in chapters 5 and 6 to compare the CPI to adversarial and accountability forms of interviewing (API).

Chapter 7 then presents an account of the more opinionated hybrid political interview (HPI), paying attention to the dimensions along which the adversarial and hybrid modalities are distinguished from each other. Chapter 8 goes on to offer a more detailed consideration of the argumentative structures of the hybrid political interview, with a focus on how journalistic standpoints such as tribuneship are managed in the context of disputes over objectivity and advocacy. Finally, chapter 9 concludes the book with an overall summary of its main arguments, and some reflections on wider aspects of the current trends in the relationship between politicians and political interviewers, and what these might mean for the future of "post-truth" journalism.

Chapter Two

Analyzing Interviews as Arenas of Language Use

Interviews are, of course, occasions of talk: talk in interaction between professional journalists and political actors of various sorts. In order to analyze in sufficient detail how language and interaction function in the specialized environment of the political interview, we need methods that will enable it to be more closely described as what Clark (1992) calls an *arena of language use*. Arenas of language use are distinct "theaters of action in which people do things with language" (Clark, 1992: xiv). This chapter outlines my approach to considering how interviews are formed as distinctive theaters of action.

Clark (1992) distinguishes between two basic approaches to the study of language use, which he calls the "product tradition" and the "action tradition." The distinction here is between approaches that focus largely on mental processes, and those that focus largely on social actions. In the product tradition, which is associated with psychology and some areas of linguistics, the aim is to understand the underlying cognitive processes which are involved in the production and understanding of language. The idea is that speaking and listening are "autonomous processes. . . . that investigators can study by looking at individuals in isolation" (Clark, 1992: xxvi).

The action tradition, on the other hand, is more concerned with observing what people actually do with language and understanding how communication is immersed in the course of interaction itself. Here, the view is that "speaking and listening are parts of collective, or joint, activities" (Clark, 1992: xxvi). In other words, investigators are interested in studying the practical accomplishment of communicating and understanding within social interaction, rather than the mental processes that lie behind it.

The analytic approach adopted within this book sits within the action tradition. I draw on the methods of conversation analysis, an approach to sociology that investigates the sequential organization of talk as a way of accessing participants' understandings of, and collaborative means of organizing, natural forms of social interaction.

CONVERSATION ANALYSIS

The field known as conversation analysis (CA) investigates the organization and orderliness of human social action through the prism of everyday talk in situations of interaction. Although it is referred to as "conversation" analysis, the forms of talk investigated, as well as the range of social contexts in which the activity of talking is examined, are not restricted to what might be thought of as everyday or casual conversation. In fact, conversation analysts refer to *speech exchange systems*, of which conversation itself is but one; and maintain that any such system, in which two or more participants exchange turns at talk for whatever purpose, can be analyzed to reveal significant detail about the organization of social life and institutions. For that reason, conversation analysts prefer to call their object of study *talk-in-interaction*:

> The term talk-in-interaction [is] prefer[red] to "conversation" so as to circumvent the connotation of triviality that has come often to be attached to the latter term, and to broaden the scope of what we mean to be dealing with to interactional settings that clearly fall outside the common-sense meaning of "conversation." (Schegloff, 2007: xiii)

The human ability to engage in talk-in-interaction is, of course, underpinned by the ability to use language in the first place. But what is at issue for CA is much greater than the structures of grammar, syntax and semantics, as these tend to be analyzed in linguistics. To study talk-in-interaction is to explore some of the most basic questions about the nature of human sociality. While there are aspects of these questions that are undoubtedly linguistic, anthropological and psychological, at the heart of the matter are some key sociological issues.

For example, talk-in-interaction is central to the organization of social life in all known human cultures. It acts as the primary medium for the establishment and maintenance of interpersonal relationships, for the exchange of information, and for the conduct of social affairs both at home and at work. Even as societies have developed technologies for mediating interpersonal communication, ranging from the letter through the telegraph, the phone call to email to Facetime and Skype, the domains of domestic and institutional life, from family mealtimes to discussions about international military strategy, continue, at root, to involve the exchange of talk-in-interaction.

Conversational activity is also one of the earliest and most important means by which children develop the linguistic skills that underpin their general social competencies. Even before they are able to understand, let alone produce, words and sentences, children understand turn-taking, routinely engaging with their caregivers in quasi-conversational exchanges of turns in both verbal and gestural formats. In developing language, children do more than simply acquire the lexis and grammar of their mother tongue. Through talk-in-interaction, they acquire the tools that afford participation as ratified members in everyday society.

And of course, talk-in-interaction is at the heart of what is happening in any media interview. There may be other things involved in the overall news item, such as a summarizing "news kernel" bulletin, a more detailed scripted report, compiled footage of relevant events or a live two-way exchange between the studio anchor and a correspondent on location (Montgomery, 2007: 39–40). But when the news item contains an interview the primary resources through which political arguments are made, probed, challenged and defended remain the exchange of turns in a speech exchange system characterized, at its base, by questions and answers.

CA originated in the work of Harvey Sacks, much of which initially appeared in the form of lectures he gave for a course on conversation that he developed at the University of California during the years 1964–72. These lectures were recorded as they were delivered, and subsequently transcribed. Sacks also collaborated closely with two other important figures in the development of the field: Emanuel Schegloff, and Gail Jefferson, who herself was the principal architect of the specialized transcription system that is used in CA (Jefferson, 2004: see Appendix). Between them these three figures published many of the foundational papers in the field (Sacks, 1963, 1972; Schegloff, 1968; Schegloff and Sacks, 1973; Sacks, Schegloff, and Jefferson, 1974; Schegloff, Jefferson, and Sacks, 1975). Jefferson's edition of Sacks's original lecture transcripts was posthumously published as a two-volume collection (Sacks, 1992).

Sacks's ideas were influenced by the form of sociology of everyday life and interpersonal behavior that Erving Goffman had developed in the 1950s (Goffman, 1956). He was also influenced by the ethnomethodology of Harold Garfinkel (Garfinkel, 1967). Sacks had a close association with Garfinkel in the early stages of his career, and the two co-authored an important paper (Garfinkel and Sacks, 1970) which drew key parallels between the methods of practical reasoning and sense-making within cultural settings (the central concern of ethnomethodology) and members' mastery of ordinary language resources as the medium for this sense-making (the central concern of CA).

Sacks was the first sociologist to take seriously the sequential organization of talk as a members' resource for contextualizing and therefore understanding situated social actions. That position was formalized in an influential paper in which the main aim is to reveal how the technical aspects of turn-taking represent structured, socially organized resources by which participants perform and coordinate activities through talk-in-interaction (Sacks, Schegloff and Jefferson, 1974). This paper contains both a generalizable model of the management of turn-taking in everyday conversation, and a theory of "speech exchange systems" by which that model can be extrapolated to other, non-conversational forms of talk-in-interaction, or so-called "institutional" discourse types.

The turn-taking model and the concept of speech exchange systems have, over the ensuing decades, provided inspiration and grounding for a vast body of work on the management of activities in everyday social interaction (Atkinson and Heritage, 1984; Lerner, 2004; Drew and Heritage, 2007) as well as on the role of talk in more specialized or formal social settings (Boden and Zimmerman, 1991; Drew and Heritage, 1992; Arminen, 2005).

In the latter kind of work (often thought of as "applied" conversation analysis) the turn-taking system for conversation is used as a benchmark against which other forms of talk-in-interaction may be recognized for their distinctiveness. Ordinary face-to-face conversation is treated, for analytic purposes, as an interactional baseline. In comparative terms, all forms of institutional interaction can be characterized by a systematic reduction and/or specialization of the array of practices observable in ordinary conversation. In such a view, the observably specialized nature of institutional discourse is therefore actively produced by participants. The upshot is that emphasis is placed not on how the setting determines the activities, strategies and procedures adopted within it, but on how those activities, strategies and procedures make available (for participants and analysts alike) participants' orientation to, and reproduction of, the setting's specialized institutional features.

ANALYZING NATURALLY-OCCURRING TALK

This way of thinking derives from CA's basic methodological standpoint, which is that in all cases analytical claims should be based on the members' own displayed understanding of their actions (Schegloff and Sacks, 1973). CA insists that is it is more important to explicate the ways that the participants in any interaction display their own understanding of what they are doing and the context in which they are doing it, than to begin from theoretically-driven assumptions about what participants may be doing or how it might be affected by pre-determined features of the context. That position evolved in the context of a critique of prevailing methodological approaches in the social and linguistic sciences; in particular, approaches in structural linguistics for which language analysis must be carried out in abstraction from actual contexts of use, and perspectives in sociology and social anthropology for which the language used by societal members is treated as a window onto the thoughts, beliefs and attitudes of sample populations.

In sociology, anthropology and related social sciences, while recent years have seen a "turn to language" in important senses, major approaches tended to view the mundane activity of talking as an unremarkable element of social life. Although it was often accepted that our capacity to use language is a major factor distinguishing humans and human society from the animal world, that capacity was not treated as a topic of analysis in its own right. Rather, sociologists and anthropologists tended to rely on language as a *resource*, providing them with access to the other phenomena they were interested in—whether external phenomena such as class, ethnicity, kinship and so on; or subjective phenomena such as people's beliefs and attitudes about such factors. The most widely adopted research methods in sociology—the interview and the questionnaire survey—and in anthropology—field observation and informant reports—still rely on language as a tool for finding out about social structures and large-scale social phenomena. But for the most part research papers render the language used in the production of their findings invisible.

Sacks, like Garfinkel, argued that members' practical reasoning about social structures should become a *topic* of analysis rather than a resource. Sacks's key insight was that members' practical reasoning becomes observable in the mundane activity of talking. Subsequently, Sacks's position has been extrapolated much more explicitly in terms of how sociological claims about the relevance of social variables must be based on the demonstrable orientations of members themselves to those variables, as displayed in the organization of talk (Schegloff, 2007).

In linguistics, a prevailing notion was that to analyze language in its most organized form, it needs to be removed from any actual instantiations in use. Many agreed with the views of Chomsky (1965), who argued that while it was possible to scientifically analyze linguistic "competence" (innate knowledge of grammatical structure that enables humans to produce meaningful sentences), the actual *use* of language ("performance") could not be scientifically described because of the disfluencies and "noise" sources that occur in natural speech. Linguistics should thus be concerned with an "ideal speaker-hearer" whose sentences were purely grammatical, and analysis was based on invented sentences, rather than utterances made by actual people in everyday contexts of language use.

Invented sentences were also used, though for practical rather than theoretical reasons, in the influential "ordinary language philosophy" of Wittgenstein (1953) and Austin (1962). However, Sacks was critical of the reliance on invented data, observing that while this approach to research can clearly yield important insights, as a method for investigating interactional uses of language it is inherently limited. This is because utterances occur not as isolated sentences but in the fluid context of conversational *sequences*. As he pointed out (Sacks, 1992, Vol. 2, 5), there is a major difference between inventing a sentence that would make sense as an utterance, and inventing a sequence of turns that one could confidently predict the occurrence of. In short, while we might feel confident in proposing that a particular sentence is grammatical or makes sense, we feel much less confident if we have to predict a sequence of turns beyond, say, a question and an answer.

So on the one hand Sacks wanted to show that everyday language, though it sometimes appears chaotic and grammatically imperfect, is nevertheless a highly ordered, socially organized phenomenon, which is therefore scientifically describable. However, he realized that one could not use intuition to understand the orderliness of ordinary conversation (or any other form of speech exchange). Rather, it was necessary to gain access somehow to the actual production of utterances in sequences, in real time.

This leads to a methodological commitment that is one of the hallmarks of CA: an emphasis on *recording* interaction in the naturally-occurring settings of social life. The use of photographic, audio and video recording technology in both the collection and analysis of data on human communication was pioneered in the 1940s and 50s by human ethologists such as Birdwhistell (1952), Bateson (1956) and Mead (Bateson and Mead, 1942), who in turn influenced researchers in facial and bodily kinesics (Scheflen and Scheflen, 1972; Kendon, 1990). Its use in the study of speech interaction was strongly advocated by conversation analysts from the beginning. Even though recordings themselves are limited in the sense that they may not capture every potentially relevant thing that occurs in and around the vicinity of the recording device, the advantages far outweigh those limitations. As Sacks put it,

> Such materials had a single virtue, that I could replay them. I could transcribe them somewhat and study them extendedly—however long it might take. The tape-recorded materials constituted a "good enough" record of what had happened. Other things, to be sure, happened, but at least what was on the tape had happened. (Sacks, 1984: 26)

All CA research is therefore based on the analysis of transcribed recordings of naturally-occurring behavior. The term "naturally-occurring behavior" refers to behavior that would have taken place whether or not the researcher intended to record it. Therefore, behavior recorded in an experimental laboratory set-up, or in an interview initiated by the researcher, falls outside this definition. But media interactions such as interviews on news programs, which would have occurred whether or not conversation analysts were interested in recording and analyzing them, do count as naturally-occurring behavior.

In fact, it might be argued that media interactions such as those analyzed in this book constitute a particularly pure type of "naturally-occurring" data. Unlike ordinary conversation, the recording of which has to involve the introduction into the setting of some kind of recording device, however unobtrusive (ten Have, 1998), the broadcast interview is recorded and transmitted over the airwaves as part of its very nature. Therefore, issues of the possible behavioral effects of the participants' awareness of the recording device (Speer and Hutchby, 2003) are of much less significance because participants enter the setting in full knowledge that their behavior will be publicly broadcast.

TURN-TAKING AND ADJACENCY PAIRS

CA's approach to sequential analysis makes it possible to examine the *co-production of mutual understanding*. Key to this is the idea of the "next turn proof procedure": namely that any "next" turn in a sequence displays its producer's understanding of the prior turn (Sacks, Schegloff and Jefferson, 1974); and by the same token, if that understanding happens to be incorrect, there are structural procedures by which that in itself can be displayed and repaired in the following turns in the sequence (Schegloff, Jefferson and Sacks, 1975).

A central CA concept that is of particular significance for the data analyzed in this book is that of "adjacency pairs" (Schegloff and Sacks, 1973). On one level this seems a fairly simple idea: certain categories of utterance make relevant a particular category of response in the next turn. Easily recognizable examples are: a greeting, which makes a return greeting relevant in the next turn; an invitation, which makes an acceptance or declination relevant in the next position; or of most relevance for us here, a question, which makes an answer relevant as the next move.

The use of the phrase "makes relevant" highlights that this pairing relationship is a social norm, rather than a causal law. The production of a first part of a pair-type, such as a question, sets up the constraint that a next speaker *should* respond by producing the relevant second part from that type—an answer. But speakers may elect *not* to provide the relevant second pair-part in their turn following a first. However, the fact that the adjacency pair relationship is normative means that, in such cases, the second speaker may be held to account, taken to task or expected to explain the absence of a relevant second pair-part; or the first speaker may seek to pursue that response.

Conversation analysts refer to this pattern by saying that a second pair-part is made *conditionally relevant* by a first pair-part. For example, as noted, motivational inferences can be drawn from the non-occurrence of a second part following the production of a first. Not returning a greeting may be taken as a sign of rudeness; not proffering a defense to an accusation may be taken as a tacit admission of guilt; not providing an answer to a question may be taken as indicative of evasiveness.

Also, the oriented-to relevance of second parts following the production of a first can remain in play across time: it is not limited to cases of literal adjacency. So whereas instances in which, say, a question is followed by another question, rather than an answer, may seem to militate against the force of the adjacency pair concept, such cases can in fact can display the temporally extendible relevance of the adjacency pair framework, once we see that the second question routinely represents a first move in an *insertion sequence* (Levinson, 1983: 304–6). Insertion sequences defer a second pair-part's production, but they do not negate its relevance. A speaker may respond to a question such as, "Can I borrow the car?" with another question: "How long do you need it?" The response to that inserted question—say, "Only a couple of hours"—provides a next slot in which a response to the first question is once more relevant and to be monitored for a response: "Okay, but remember I need it later."

A further aspect of the normative properties of adjacency pairs lies in the systematically different ways that recipients of first parts design the alternative actions to be done in second position. Invitations, for instance, can be accepted or declined; requests can be granted or rejected. The significant point is that these alternatives are *non-equivalent*. That non-equivalence is traced in the features of turn design through which alternative second parts are proffered. Broadly, responses which agree or are congruent with the expectation projected by a first pair-part are produced contiguously and without mitigation. Responses which diverge from that expectation—which in some way disagree—tend to be prefaced by hesitations, discourse markers such as "Well . . . ," and, unlike congruent responses, are accompanied by accounts for why the speaker is responding in this way (Sacks, 1987).

These different response types are termed *preferred* and *dispreferred* respectively. Importantly, the concept of preference in CA is not used to refer to the internal psychological dispositions of individuals, but to point to this structural feature of turn design in some types of adjacency pair (Pomerantz, 1984). Research has additionally shown that the design features of dispreferred responses can be used as a resource for the maintenance of social solidarity in talk-in-interaction. This is so not only in the way that dispreferred responses may be accompanied by accounts or explanations; but also in the way that hesitations and other means of marking a dispreferred response can provide a source for a first speaker to revise the original first pair-part in such a way as to try and avoid disagreement or rejection (Davidson, 1984).

The adjacency pair concept has been important in studying the distinctive methods of turn-taking and activity organization found in settings other than ordinary conversation, such as courts of law (Atkinson and Drew, 1979), school classrooms (McHoul, 1978), radio and television talk shows (Hutchby, 1996, 2006), doctors' surgeries (Heath, 1992; Maynard and Heritage, 2004), and many others (Drew and Heritage, 1992); including, of course, broadcast news interviews (Clayman and Heritage, 2002).

To conclude this brief introduction to CA, and provide an initial sense of how the method and its conceptual framework will be applied in the following analyses of broadcast political interviews, I will give an outline of what has come to be described by many as the more applied wing of conversation analysis.

CA AND INSTITUTIONAL DISCOURSE

In studies of "institutional" behavioral settings, CA has developed a distinctive perspective on how participants themselves play a central role in establishing and reproducing the context-specific nature of their interaction. At root, this is based on the idea that different forms of talk can be understood on a continuum ranging from the relatively unconstrained turn-taking of mundane conversation, through various levels of formality, to ceremonial occasions in which not only who speaks and in what sequential order, but also what they will say, are pre-arranged: for instance, in wedding ceremonies (Sacks et al, 1974). By selectively reducing or otherwise transforming the full scope of conversational practices, concentrating on some and withholding others, participants can be seen to display an orientation to particular institutional norms as relevant for their current state of interaction. In many institutional settings, including the broadcast news interview, "the institutional character of the interaction is embodied first and foremost in its *form*—most notably in turn-taking systems which depart substantially from the way in which turn-taking is managed in conversation" (Heritage and Greatbatch, 1991: 95).

The earliest news interview research began by focusing on the ways in which participants orient to a turn-taking format which centrally involves chains of question-answer-next question sequences (Greatbatch, 1988). Within this framework, journalists were found to adopt forms of "neutralistic" grammar that enable them to formulate probing or challenging questions without taking up positions in their own right (Clayman, 1992), while politicians and other public figures use careful or highly circumspect means of taking up—or avoiding taking up—positions on topics of key public interest (Greatbatch, 1986; Harris, 1991; Bull, 2008). This is, of course, very different from turn-taking in mundane conversation, where roles are not restricted to those of questioner and answerer, and where the type and order of turns in a given interaction may vary quite freely. During the course of an interview, normative rules operate which mean that attempts to move outside the boundaries of the question-answer framework may be subject to sanction.

The existence of such unspoken, or tacit rules can be seen particularly clearly when, for whatever reason, one or another participant ceases to observe the convention that interviewers should put questions and interviewees answer them. In the following example the interviewee begins accusing the interviewer of misrepresenting him in a previous broadcast and demands to know why, while the interviewer overtly requests that the interviewee observe the norms by allowing him to play the "interviewer" role (for a description of the transcription conventions, see Appendix):

```
(1)  (Greatbatch, 1988: 421-2) IR = Interviewer, IE = Interviewee

1      IE:    despite the fact there were fou:r major factories
2             that you knew about,=despite the fact there was a two
3             hundred and thirty million capital investment programme
4             that you knew about,=.hhh that we dealt in companies you
5             stated and restated toda::y, .hhh despite the fact that
6             ninety one per cent of our companies are still there:,=
7             and only the marginal ones which you knew were sold, .hhh
8             and you e:ven mislead people by suggesting for instance
9             that we owned the Parisian publishing house Brooke.
10→           Why.=
11     IR:    =s-s-s-Sir James I['m so sorry (     ) I'm so s-
12     IE:                     [No,=I'm asking a question now.=
```

```
13→  IR:   =It's more conventional in these programmes [fo:r

14   IE:                                                [Well I

15         don't mind ab[out    convention. = ]I'm asking you why

16→  IR:                [me to ask questions,]

17         (.)

18   IE:   you distorted those facts.
```

The interviewer (IR) even states, in line 13, that it is "conventional" that he should ask the questions, while the interviewee (IE) explicitly disregards that convention (line 14–15) and persists in attempting to ask a question of his own.

By showing that the tacit rules governing the turn-taking structure can be actively brought into play by both IR and IE if they are breached, we can see, in line with the CA approach, that the characteristic question-answer structure of the interview is actively oriented to and ongoingly accomplished by the participants, rather than some invisible causal force that determines their behavior outside of their awareness. The interview's rules of engagement are, in short, like a game of chess or checkers: actively known about, oriented to and ongoingly managed by the participants in their behavioral choices (Garfinkel, 1967).

This more applied wing of CA acts as one type of challenge to some of the critiques that have come from within sociology and linguistics. One critical argument is that CA lacks an adequate sense of the contextualization of utterances within a wider set of social relations. A second, related claim has been that CA in general is unwilling to make links between the micro details of talk-in-interaction and the macro levels of sociological variables—class, gender, power relations, ideologies, cultural values and so forth.

Such critiques are fueled by the fact that much CA scholarship, especially in the earlier years, can come across as reluctant to engage explicitly with sociological concepts such as power, gender, class, and so on. Partly, this has to do with its theoretical lineage. As noted, CA emerged in the context of a critique of conventional sociological thinking which sees talk mainly as a resource for demonstrating the existence of macro-level phenomena (power, gender, class, etc.) that, for sociological theorizing, inevitably affect people's behavior. For instance, a characteristic claim might be that "our social practice in general and our use of language in particular are bound up with causes and effects which we may not be at all aware of under normal conditions" (Fairclough, 1995: 54). Another might be that social institutions "are characterized by . . . hierarchical relations of power between the occupants of institutional positions," and, consequently, in their actions institutional agents "exercise the power which is institutionally endowed upon them" (Thompson, 1984: 165).

For CA, such views simplify the question considerably. Rather than taking it for granted that unconscious causes or power relations determine the course of encounters, CA aims to describe the ways that participants display their active awareness of—or orientation to—context-specific factors, in and through the design of their talk. By focusing on the local management of talk-in-interaction, the CA approach can provide compelling, but differently structured, accounts of how power comes to operate as a feature of, and is used as a resource in, institutional interaction. The question, in short, becomes one of *how* participants manage role-related distributions of interactional resources to achieve effects that are differentially available to others in the setting (Hutchby, 1996).

Here again, the question-answer sequence turns out to be central (Drew and Heritage, 1992). In many forms of institutional interaction, questions do indeed get asked primarily by institutional figures, such as attorneys, doctors, and news interviewers. Questions are a powerful interactional resource for the simple reason that the asking of a question places constraints on the discourse options available to its recipient. And while individual questions constrain, sequences of questions can constrain more strongly.

For example, in Atkinson and Drew's (1979) courtroom studies, the fact that the attorney is able to ask sequences of questions which the witness is restricted to answering gives particular powers to the attorney. One of these is what Drew (1992) later described as the "power of summary." The questioner "has 'first rights' to pull together evidence and 'draw conclusions'"; in other words, to define the meaning and the terms of a particular set of answers, which is something that the witness cannot do. "The witness is left in a position of addressing and trying to deal with the attorney's selection of which items to pull together: she has no control over the connections which are made. . . . nor over the inferences which may be drawn from such juxtapositioning" (Drew, 1992: 507).

In such a formal type of institutional interaction, the normative constraints that inform participants' actions are severe, and there may be particular consequences of breaking them (for example, "contempt of court"). In more informal settings, institutional figures may not have the support of such sanctions in their role of asking the questions. This in itself can have distinctive consequences for relations of power within institutional encounters. For instance, studies of doctor-patient interaction have shown how patients, by *withholding* talk at certain points in a diagnostic sequence, may be complicit in the construction and maintenance of a power situation in which the doctor not only determines the topics that will be talked about, but also defines the upshots and outcomes of their discussions (Frankel, 1984; Heath, 1992; Maynard and Heritage, 2004).

Thus, by showing how participants display an orientation to institutional settings by engaging in certain activities and refraining from others, and illustrating how activities such as questioning are used to constrain the options of a coparticipant, CA can be used to demonstrate how power comes to be a feature of those activities. Oriented-to activity patterns, such as differences in questioning and answering moves, may themselves be intrinsic to the play of power in institutional interactions.

In short, CA is not entirely resistant to linking the properties of talk with higher-level sociological variables. But CA is resistant to *assuming* linkages between the properties of talk and higher-level sociological variables. The debate between CA and sociology more widely is not about the *existence* of factors such as power in interaction. Rather, it is an argument about the nature of claims that can legitimately be made about the data we gather to analyze language use in social interaction.

Chapter Three

Total Mediatization

A Media Ecology of the Broadcast Political Interview

Although the main focus of the book is on the form of talk-in-interaction that occurs in the broadcast interview, interviews themselves are not stand-alone events taking place in a discursive vacuum. The broadcast interview plays a part in a much wider ecology of mediatized political discourses to which it is reflexively related. In this chapter I continue the discussion of "total mediatization" by considering some features of this wider ecology.

In chapter 1, I quoted Clayman and Heritage's (2002: 25) remark that news interviews may have "ramifications for personal careers, for public affairs, and sometimes for the march of history." As a range of work has shown, these ramifications derive from the way in which interviews are, simultaneously, routine television and radio events, and happenings with potentially unpredictable consequences that are bound up in a wider discursive ecology of news in the current era of political mediatization (Bull et al., 2014; Clayman, 1995; Ekström, 2001; Eriksson and Östman, 2013). In various ways, the talk that is produced within a news interview can subsequently be re-contextualized and re-mediated by numerous agencies, including journalists themselves, producers and editors of broadcast news programs, and related news media, including the press and, increasingly, in contemporary times, the internet and social media.

This remediation of politicians' words in interviews is often undertaken in the pursuit of controversial or newsworthy reportage. For example, in news bulletins that do not themselves feature extended live interviews, producers may cut single answers from longer interviews and, stripped of their context in the question-answer sequence of the interview, incorporate them into news stories (Eriksson, 2011) or stitch together different interview utterances to create what appear to be dialogs on current topics (Ekström, 2001). Similarly, in the soundbite culture of modern news broadcasting, it is commonplace for single utterances to be extracted, quoted, disseminated and interpreted elsewhere in the media as "defining moments" that come to epitomize a story or political position (Clayman, 1995).

Increasingly, in what Chadwick (2014) has called the hybrid media system, not only is contemporary political action enveloped by media scrutiny, but the technological forms of mediation are diversified rather than concentrated. Rather than the relatively homogeneous and sometimes slow-moving spheres of the press and the scheduled broadcast news bulletin, anything that politicians do or say, including what they e-mail, tweet, blog, and the rest, is nowadays subject to scrutiny and potential newsworthiness across an intertwined range of media outlets including social networking and other internet resources as well as the conventional forms of mass communication, which themselves transcend the limitations of schedules through non-stop broadcasting and web-based newspapers.

To take just one example of the consequences of this: some years ago British politician Emily Thornberry was forced to resign from her role as shadow Attorney General in the Labour Party after a tweet in which she posted a picture of a white van parked in the drive of a suburban house in Rochdale with St. George flags hanging from the windows. Here, the semiotics of the British class system became central in the widespread remediation of a single tweet. In England, both the white Ford Transit van and the flag of St. George (the English flag, as distinct from the Union Jack) have become cultural signifiers for a particular type of white, male, working class figure whose political views are stereotypically right-wing and nationalist: "White Van Man." Although the tweet itself was careful not to make such a connection explicit, the picture was interpreted on Twitter and elsewhere within the social media as a sneering caricature of the English working class. It may seem a relatively inconsequential event, but three years later when Thornberry stood as a candidate for the leadership of her party, the gaffe was revivified as she was pressed, in a BBC spotlight interview, about how it reflected her character.

This chapter broadens our understanding of the media ecology of political interview discourse by means of a comparative study of three further examples of re-mediated talk by politicians, in each of which an interview plays a central, but differing, role in the construction of what becomes publicly and colloquially known as a gaffe.

Gaffes, at least as they originate in news interviews, centrally involve what I will call "infelicitous talk," a term referring to something said in the public sphere that is either ill-advised or wrong, or may in fact be a genuine attempt to answer a difficult question, but crucially is subsequently *construed* as problematic, resulting in intensified media interest, usually over a concentrated period of time such as a few days. In various ways, that infelicitous talk is then re-mediated, disseminated, interpreted and reformulated through other media outlets. This process leads the politician to embarrassment, controversy, and sometimes even resignation from public office. It is the different ways in which this process happens, and the different media configurations involved, that is the focus of attention in what follows.

The chapter analyzes the changing relationship between interview conduct and the wider media ecology through the prism of three interview-based political gaffes that occurred between the pre-internet days of the 1980s and the more recent, hybrid media times. Common features of the three selected events include that they all involved incumbent leaders of the British Labour Party; that they all centrally involved conduct during a broadcast interview (though the type of interview and its context differs in each case); and that they were all represented elsewhere in the media as bearing direct consequences for the public perception of the leadership qualities of the politician in question.

Of course, it is not only Labour Party politicians who may be prone to gaffes in the British context. I have chosen this particular set of gaffe-producers on the basis of a common perception that the majority of the British press favor a conservative or right-wing standpoint, and it might therefore be argued that Labour Party leaders—particularly those considered to be left-wing—face a more hostile media environment in which gaffes can become more consequential.

However, it is not necessarily the gaffes themselves that are the central interest. As we will see, each of the events differs in terms of the array of media technologies that were involved in evaluating interview conduct in the wider ecology. It is these differences that in turn show how contemporary conditions of total mediatization are becoming increasingly difficult to manage for political actors.

MEDIATIZED COMMUNICATION AND THE POLITICAL GAFFE

In conditions of total mediatization, a constant danger for politicians is that any statement which may be, to use the spin doctors' phrase, "off-message" can be picked up and turned into a reportable phenomenon—a gaffe. One consequence of this is that political figures, and their communications managers, are extraordinarily cautious about what they say in interviews. They know that not only interviewers, but other journalists working for other media outlets, are scrutinizing their statements for mistakes that can be turned into reportable phenomena. This cautiousness, in turn, can lead to different kinds of problems in the political interview, such as perceptions of evasiveness or refusing to answer a straight question, an issue we will return to later.

Gaffes are not necessarily scandalous. In their work on media and political scandal, both Thompson (2000) and Ekström and Johanssen (2008) distinguish gaffes from scandals on the grounds that not every gaffe becomes a full-blown scandal; and indeed, some gaffes may remain relatively inconsequential. Nevertheless, Thompson's statement that political scandals are "events which are constituted in part by mediated forms of communication" (2000: 61) can be equally applied to our understanding of political gaffes.

Of course, gaffes do not only occur as a result of interview conduct (cf. the Thornberry tweet, above). Infelicitous talk can appear in private communications intended for restricted audiences; but if these are leaked to the press it can result in serious consequences. A well-known historical example in the British context is the statement by a government communications officer, Jo Moore, that the events of September 11th, 2001, represented "a good day for burying bad news"—that is, for releasing stories that might reflect negatively on the government, because they would pass unnoticed in comparison to the magnitude of the terrorist attacks on the World Trade Center. Originally appearing in an e-mail circulated to press office staff, the leaked comment was filtered through subsequent press reports and interviews and became a subject of intense media scrutiny. The resultant furor led to a press campaign of vilification against Ms. Moore; to her appearance on a television news program in which she offered her apologies for making the statement; and ultimately, following a later incident in which she was accused, falsely as it turned out, of seeking to bury more bad news, to her resignation.

Moore's statement was undoubtedly ill-advised, though it had not originally been intended for wider public distribution. A similar type is the "open mic" gaffe in which a politician is caught in infelicitous talk without realizing that a microphone was switched on. Another famous historical example, this time from the US context, is the joke announcement made by President Ronald Reagan in 1984 during a soundcheck prior to one of his regular National Public Radio addresses. Speaking, as he thought, off-mic while radio technicians were busy preparing the broadcast, President Reagan parodied the opening lines of his planned speech, saying, "My fellow Americans, I'm pleased to tell you today that I've signed legislation that will outlaw Russia forever. We begin bombing in five minutes." Not surprisingly, due to the president's status as chief authority over the largest nuclear arsenal on the planet, this joke became an internationally reported gaffe that led to condemnatory statements from the Russian government. (The second case discussed below also involves an open mic gaffe.)

Once the broadcast interview goes live, a different set of dynamics is in play because while the interviewee is on air, his or her speech must be treated as "knowingly, wittingly public" (Scannell, 1991: 11). In such a situation, it may seem, intentional infelicities such as Reagan's would not occur due to the interviewee's awareness that they were being heard by the audience. Nevertheless, gaffes can sometimes be created entirely by media reaction to a politician's utterance. In other words, the politician may feel that he or she is choosing their words very carefully—particularly if the issue in question is a controversial one—but the media logic that comes into operation can construct a reading of those words that is quite different from what was originally intended. This is the case in the first of my examples.

GAFFE CONFIGURATION 1: TELEVISION AND THE PRESS

This example of the media's constitutive role in re-mediating infelicitous talk involves an event in 1987: an era in which the only major outlets for mediatized political representation were the print newspapers and broadcasting. Here, then, the ecological relationship in which the gaffe was cultivated is between the two media technologies that dominated the twentieth-century political landscape.

In the late 1980s the British Labour Party, while in opposition, had adopted an official policy of unilateral nuclear disarmament. In the run-up to the 1987 election, leader Neil Kinnock was pressed on the reasoning behind the policy, and in one televised interview he was asked what he would do, as prime minister, if a non-nuclear Britain were threatened by an aggressor who possessed nuclear weapons. Such a question is of course loaded, in that it carries the strong implication that a nuclear force is inherently more powerful than a non-nuclear one, and therefore it would seem that the latter would be unable to resist attack or invasion by the former.

The difficult task facing Kinnock was to construct an answer to the question that neither acknowledged the interviewer's loaded implication, nor admitted that there may be a weakness in his party's nuclear disarmament policy. Kinnock's answer was as follows:

(1) TVN: Neil Kinnock (From Garton et al., 1991: 102)

1	Kinnock:	In those circumstances, the choice is again
2		posed – and this is the classical choice – of
3		either exterminating everything you stand for
4		and, I'll use the phrase 'the flower of your

5	youth', or using resources you've got to
6	make any occupation totally intenable,
7	untenable. And of course, any effort to
8	occupy Western Europe, or certainly to
9	occupy the United Kingdom, would be utterly
10	untenable and any potential force knows that
11	very well and are not going to be ready to
12	engage in attempting to dominate conditions
13	that they couldn't dominate.

As Bull (2008) observes, political interviewers often aim to construct questions to which the politician's attempt to provide an answer will inevitably appear evasive and slippery. This is what happens in this case. Kinnock's attempts to be cautious come across as vague: he argues that "resources" would be mobilized to make the occupation "untenable" but without saying what the resources are. He implies, though with no supporting evidence, that because "any potential force" knows that an attack would "be utterly untenable," they would not even try it.

Of course, the reason for this vagueness is because his own party's policy, of which he had been a key architect, placed him in an almost impossible situation. As the leader of the party he must defend the policy, but it is relatively easy for the opposing party to argue that having abandoned its nuclear arsenal under a future Labour government, Britain would be unable to defend against an attack by any nation threatening to use nuclear weapons. Although he tried to construct a genuine answer to the question, therefore, potentially any answer Kinnock gave could turn out to be politically dangerous.

In a detailed analysis of the following day's newspapers, Garton, Montgomery and Tolson (1991) show how Kinnock's phrase "using the resources you've got to make any occupation totally. . . . untenable" became constructed as an example of infelicitous talk. Journalists used quotations gleaned from political opponents to render this position equivalent to "a policy of surrender" (George Younger, Conservative politician, quoted in the *Daily Telegraph*, 25 May 1987), "an invitation to attack" (Michael Heseltine, Conservative politician, quoted in the *Daily Express*, 25 May 1987) and "as if the Mujahideen in Penge High Street were expected to deter Soviet nuclear blackmail" (John Cartwright, Conservative politician, quoted in the *Daily Telegraph*, 25 May 1987). The latter quote was particularly significant for the way that Kinnock's answer became construed as a gaffe in subsequent news reporting, with its reference to the guerilla forces who, through highly trained and Western government–supported warfare in difficult mountainous territory (as opposed to the idiomatically suburban "Penge High Street"), played a major role in defeating the Soviet army during the 1979–89 war in Afghanistan.

The construction of Kinnock's gaffe became complete with the headline of the *Daily Telegraph* the day after the interview was broadcast: "GUERILLA WAR A DETERRENT SAYS KINNOCK" (*Daily Telegraph*, 25 May 1987). Although, as we can see from extract (1), Kinnock did not use the term "guerilla war," the significance is that once these interpretations of what he did say were projected into the public sphere, the actual words which Kinnock used, as well as his actual meaning, were lost and the agenda became set by the *Daily Telegraph*'s formulation. Once that happened, Kinnock was forced to respond to, and defend, a claim which, from his point of view, he had never explicitly made.

Thus, Kinnock's somewhat slippery attempt to answer a question which, however he chose to answer it, was designed to cause a political problem for him, ended up yielding an example of infelicitous talk: talk that is inappropriate or unfortunate in its setting. In this case, the technological configuration of the remediation of that talk is fairly straightforward, involving a transposition from television broadcast, through journalist consultations with opposition politicians, to newspaper headline. Other, more recent examples are far more complex.

GAFFE CONFIGURATION 2: TV, RADIO, THE PRESS, THE TAPE, AND THE NET

The second example occurred in 2010, and this time involved an incumbent Labour prime minister, Gordon Brown, who had already been embroiled in a media scandal based on leaked information from inside his own offices, known as "bullygate" (Chadwick, 2011). The configuration of infelicitous talk in this case involved wireless outside broadcast technology, a radio interview, a tape recording of a private conversation, and internet sites such as YouTube; and highlights the rapidity of news evolution in the modern era of live rolling news.

During a live television interview Brown was giving while on an election campaign visit to Rochdale, in northern England, a voter had begun calling out, voicing her concerns (shared by many in Britain at the time) about the national debt. Eventually the prime minister's aides decided that having him be seen to engage with the kind of concerns expressed by the woman (later named as Gillian Duffy) would provide good evidence of his connection with

38   *Chapter Three*

the public mood. Brown initially made well-intentioned efforts to respond to Mrs. Duffy's complaints about education, taxation and immigration. The latter issue, however, became escalated, with Mrs. Duffy at one point asking, "And all these eastern European [immigrants], where are they flocking from?"—the word "flocking" having distinct connotations of some kind of coordinated mass influx. She went on to indicate that the government's policies on these matters had led her to change her mind about voting for Brown's party. Nonetheless, the exchange ended with the prime minister wishing Mrs. Duffy and her family well as she turned away.

As he left the scene in his chauffeured car, heading to Manchester for an interview with the BBC, Brown discussed this encounter with a political aide travelling with him. At this point the television cameras had been left behind and Brown, thinking himself off-air, referred to the encounter as "ridiculous" and to Mrs. Duffy as a "bigoted woman" (see extract 2 below). It turned out, however, that his lapel microphone was still switched on and the radio signal was still being received in the outside broadcast truck. The recording made by the engineers on location would shortly come back to haunt Gordon Brown, some arguing that this moment marked a watershed in the election campaign that he subsequently lost (Porter and Prince, 2010).

Later the same day, two further encounters were broadcast that were to cement the event in the public consciousness, as what became known as the "bigotgate" controversy unfolded. In one, Gordon Brown was in the studio giving his pre-arranged news interview on BBC radio's Jeremy Vine show. In the second, on-location reporters and camera crews had caught up with Gillian Duffy at the scene of the earlier exchange. Having heard the comments made in the official limousine, they interviewed her about her reaction to being called a bigot by the prime minister. Both the conversation between Brown and Vine in the studio, and that between Mrs. Duffy and reporters, were broadcast live, on the BBC and Sky News respectively.

The BBC interview takes place about an hour after the encounter with Mrs. Duffy, and although it is broadcast live, Brown speaks via a link from a studio in Manchester while Vine is in the BBC's London studio. The interview as a whole is thirty minutes long and for the first twenty-seven minutes, Vine presses the prime minister in some detail about the current recession and the global financial crisis. Three minutes before the end, he switches tack to raise the Gillian Duffy encounter, revealing that he has been briefed about the newsworthy "bigoted woman" quote (lines 6–7), but not the fuller content of the exchange (lines 3–5). As Brown (IE in the transcript below) produces his apologetic response (lines 9–16), Vine (IR) introduces a fairly direct remediation of the original event, by announcing that someone has "handed [him] the tape" (line 17).

(2) R2: Vine-Brown

```
1     IR:    Can I ask you about a voter you've just met
2            apparently on the way to us:, this is a woman
3            called Gillian Duffy who:, .hh I think was just
4            questioning you about tuition fees an' a
5            couple of other thin:gs, .hh a:n:d, as you
6            went away a microphone picked you up saying
7            that was, a very bigoted woman. Is that what
8            you [said.
9     IE:        [.Mhht I apologise if I've said anything like
10           that eh w-what I think she was raising with me
11           was a- was an issue about eh immigration and
12           saying that there were too many um e:::r people
13           from eastern Europe in the country and err I do
14           apologise if I've said anything that's been
15           hu-hurtful and I will apologise to her
16           personally.=
17→   IR:    =Someone has just handed me the tape let's- play
18           it and see if we can hear it.

TAPE ((Muffled: Sounds of car engine in background)):

19    Brown:  Should never have put me with that-
20            with that woman.(0.5) Whose idea
21            was that.
22    Aide:   Don't know I didn't see.
23    Brown:  Was Sue I think. (1.2) J's ridiculous.
24            (1.8)
25    Aide:   They've said that- that actually- (0.3)
26            they're not sure if they'll go with
27            that one.=
```

```
28   Brown:   =They will go with it.
29            (1.2)
30   Aide:    What did she say.
31   Brown:   Achh ev'rything, she's just this sort of,
32            bigoted woman. (0.4) said she used to be
33            Labour.
```

STUDIO:

```
34   IR:   Thu-that is: w-what you said. .h Er:m, is sh-she
35         not allowed to express her view [to you or what.
36   IE:                                   [Of course she's
37         allowed to express her view an' I was saying
38         that.=The prob- the problem was, that erm, I:
39         was dealing with a question that she raised about
40         erm, immigration an' I wasn't given a chance te
41         answer it because, we had a whole melee of press
42         around her=but u-of course I apologise if I've
43         said anything that 'as .hhhhh that 'as been
44         offensive an' I would never, put myself in a
45         position where I would want tuh, to say anything
46         er like that about a- u-er v- er- er a woman I- a-
47         a woman I met.=i- it w-was a question about=um:
48         immigration that really eh eh I think was
49         annoying.
50   IR:   And you're blaming a member of your sta:ff there
51         Sue is [it,
52   IE:          [No I'm blaming myself and er: I blame
53         myself for what is- what is done but, you gotta
54         remember that this was me being helpful to the
55         broadcasters with eh, .hh with my microphone on,
56         ehw- rushing into the ca:r because I had to get
```

```
57            to another appointment and er, .hhh e:r they 've
58            chosen to play eh, my private conversation with
59            er with- the person who was in the car with me.
60            Er I- I know these things can happen I-I-I I
61            apologise profusely to the- to the lady concerned
62            .hhhh I don't think she is, u-er that I think it
63            was jus:t, (.) the view that she expressed that
64            I was worried about that I couldn't respond to.
```

Unlike the transcript in extract (1), what we see in this transcript is the interactional context in which the interview participants each produce their talk. The news interview is, at root, a question-and-answer turn-taking system (chapter 4), and here we see Vine putting three questions to the prime minister. Vine's questions, in line with what has been his strategy throughout the interview so far, seek to have the prime minister admit personal responsibility for a political misjudgment: first by asking Brown to admit whether or not he said that Mrs. Duffy was a bigoted woman (line 6–8); second by implying that Brown is seeking to dismiss or deny Mrs. Duffy's right to express an opinion (line 34–35); and third by suggesting that Brown is seeking to deflect responsibility to one of his staff ("Sue is it," line 50–51).

Within this context of seeking to establish personal responsibility, and within the question-answer framework of the interview, somewhat uniquely, the tape itself comes to be allocated a "turn." Vine inserts the taped words into the live broadcast interaction between himself and his interviewee. It is not clear whether he, or anyone else on the production team, has actually heard the tape at this point; but his phrase "Someone has just handed me the tape let's play it and see if we can hear it" (line 17–18) suggests that Vine, at least, has not. However, the playing of the tape allows Vine, in the exchange that follows its playing, to utilize Brown's words in order to construct his line of questioning.

At the moment Vine plays the tape, then, Brown's gaffe is made concrete as his private words now become public, broadcast talk. Moreover, unlike in most other instances in which political gaffes unfold in the media, Brown himself is made witness to his own infelicitous talk, sitting in the studio listening to his supposedly private comments become public material. And Vine can use those words as a resource ("Thu-that is: w-what you said." line 34) in his attempt to establish Brown's personal responsibility for a political misjudgment (which Brown, in fact, accepts in his turn beginning on line 52).

As noted, this interview was broadcast on radio, which meant of course that Brown was not visible to the audience at the time. However, it turns out, compounding the prime minister's problems, that these days live video feeds of popular radio programs are often streamed via the internet. Footage from this live feed, subsequently posted on YouTube, shows Brown with his head in his hands as he listens to the tape recording that Vine is broadcasting.

Not only was Brown, like Kinnock in the previous example, subsequently forced to account for himself under intensive scrutiny in the press and broadcast media; the mediatization of his gaffe also took place via the internet and social networking. With sites such as YouTube, Twitter, Facebook, Instagram, WhatsApp, and the rest, an ever-widening sphere of public access to, and debate about, the remediation of the gaffe comes into play. Not only was the video footage of Brown's interview with Vine posted on YouTube, but also the original televised footage of his interview with Gillian Duffy, and the recording of her subsequent interview with Sky television reporters, in which she is shown in open-mouthed shock at the reporter's recounting of the prime minister's description of her as bigoted. Thus, even those who missed the original media event (a much larger group than those who may have been watching Sky News or listening to Radio 2 at the time) now have direct access to the event via their computers. And, of course, web technology enables all of this to be subjected to extensive and often only minimally regulated, or indeed unregulated, commentary from members of the public (Thornborrow, 2014).

This widening of the sphere of total mediatization is something that can also be exploited by journalists themselves, in their attempts to report on events outside the constraints placed on them by political communications managers. My final example illustrates how this, too, can result in the construction and remediation of infelicitous talk.

GAFFE CONFIGURATION 3: TV, THE PRESS, THE NET, BLOGGERY AND TWEETERY

In 2011, British public sector workers were engaged in a dispute with the government over their pay and pensions provision, which were under the control of the treasury rather than private pensions companies. Labour politician Ed Miliband, who had just taken over leadership of his party and was soon to be standing in a general election, gave a television interview to outline his position on the strike campaign that the public sector unions had just announced.

Miliband's aim in this interview was to express his opposition to the strikes, on the grounds that negotiations between the Conservative/Liberal coalition government and the unions were still ongoing. In order to achieve this, Miliband faced a problem similar to that faced by his predecessor Neil Kinnock, discussed above. He led a party that had originally been established by the trades unions, that professed to be the party of the workers as opposed to the Conservatives, who were seen as the party of business, and in which the trades unions still wielded enormous power through the number of votes they controlled in key policy decisions, including the election of party leaders.

Miliband's strategy in walking the line between aligning himself with the significant proportion of the voting population who were opposed to the idea that teachers, nurses and firefighters should go on strike, and risking the wrath of unions and striking workers themselves, who would see him as their natural advocate, was to engage in a highly controlled interview aimed at creating a soundbite for dissemination across the news networks. As the data will show, the soundbite was to have been something like Mr. Miliband saying: "These strikes are wrong, at a time when negotiations are still going on."

In fact, Miliband posted exactly this soundbite on his Twitter feed: "These strikes are wrong at a time when negotiations are going on. People have been let down by both sides—the Govt has acted recklessly" (twitter, @ed_miliband, 30.6.2011). And the BBC News website included the soundbite in its report at the time:

> The Labour leader Ed Miliband has expressed his disapproval at both the unions and the government over the strike action taking place around the UK. Picket lines have been set up by public sector workers, to protest at planned pension changes, resulting in the closure of almost half of state schools across the UK. Mr. Miliband said, "these strikes are wrong at a time when negotiations are going on", but refused to elaborate when asked further questions. (https://www.bbc.co.uk/news/av/uk-politics-13971770, 30.6.2011).

The interview subsequently became notorious because of two things: first, the means by which Miliband's communication managers sought to ensure that the soundbite would be clear enough to be picked up by the mainstream media; and second, the way that their techniques of doing so were subsequently revealed to public view via other media such as Twitter, YouTube and internet blogging.

As we see in the following transcript (produced from the extended footage the BBC posted on its news website), the strategy was for there to be a series of about four memorized phrases that together encapsulated the intended message. Miliband simply reproduced the same set of phrases, in slightly different order, in response to each of the questions the interviewer put to him.

For ease of reference I will split the interview into segments. Extract (3) shows the initial statement made by Mr. Miliband. The question to which this is probably a response was not broadcast, a common strategy in news reporting (Clayman 1990). The subsequent extracts show the four follow-up questions that do in fact appear on the recording.

```
(3) Pool: Miliband Part 1

1    IE:   These strikes are wrong, at a time when negotiations
2          are still going on. .hh Our parents an' the public
3          ev been let down by both si:des, .h because the
4          government es acted in a reckless, an' provocative
5          m-manner. (0.2) After today's disruption, I urge
6          both si:des, (.) t' put aside the rhetoric, (.) get
7          round the negotiating table, and stop it happening
8          again.
```

Here we find the four central points Miliband wishes to convey: the strikes are wrong because negotiations are ongoing; parents and the public have been let down by both sides in the dispute; the government has acted recklessly and provocatively; and both sides should put aside their rhetoric and get round the negotiating table. As the interviewer puts a set of questions which seek to expand on Miliband's statement from various angles, it is noticeable that these four central points are reiterated with only slight modifications that make them appear to act as answers to the questions.

First, the interviewer seeks to press Miliband on the problematic issue that many of his own supporters actually make up the striking workforce that he appears to be criticizing. In response, Miliband repeats his points, but in a different order than extract (3) (line 16ff).

```
(4) Pool: Miliband Part 2

9    IR:   .HHhm E:rm, u-I: listened t'your speech in Wrexham
10         you talked about the Labour Party being a movement=a
11         lotta people in that movement, .h e::r are people
12         who're on strike toda:y an' they'll be looking at
13         you an' thinking well, .hh you're describing these
14         strikes as wro:ng. Why aren't you giving us more
```

```
15            leadership as the leader of the labour movement.
16     IE:    .hh At a time when negotiations are still going
17            o:n, I do believe these stri:kes, are wrong. .h An'
18            that's why I say, both sides, should after today's
19            disruption, get round the negotiating table, .h put
20            aside the rhetoric, .h an' sort the problem out.
21            .h Because the public an' parents ev been let down
22            by both sides, .h=the goverment's acted in a
23            reckless an' provocative manner.
```

Next, the interviewer asks whether Miliband considers the negotiations themselves to be in good faith. Again, rather than answering that particular question, Miliband repeats his list of central propositions in a different order (this time omitting the point about public and parents being let down).

```
(5) Pool: Miliband Part 3
24     IR:    .hhMHh Well I spoke to Francis Maude before I
25            came here and, the tone he was striking was a very
26            conciliatory one..hh D'you think there's a
27            difference between the words they're saying in
28            public an' the attitude they're striking in
29            private in these negotiations=Are their
30            negotiations in good faith would you say.
31     IE:    .hh What I say is that the strikes are wrong when
32            negotiations er still going on. .h=But the
33            government has acted in a reckless and provocative
34            manner. .h=in the way it's gone about these
35            issu:es. .h A:fter today's disruption I urge
36            both sides to get round the negotiating table,
37            put aside the rhetoric, an' stop this kinda thing
38            happening again.
```

In the final two questions, the interviewer seeks to press Miliband on whether he has expressed his views on a personal level to the key negotiators in the government and the unions (lines 39–45); and subsequently, on whether he has a view on how the disruption might affect parents on an everyday level, including within that category both himself and Mr. Miliband (line 54–55: "You're a parent I'm a parent, lotta people watching this will be parents.") Once more, between lines 46 and 53, and lines 61 and the interview's end in line 70, the answers consist of the four central propositions reiterated in slightly different order.

```
(6) Pool: Miliband Part 4
39    IR:   Er:m, it's a s- it's a- it's a:- it's a statement
40          you've made, er publicly=an' you've made it to
41          me=an' obviously this will be broadca:st
42          obvislee=but have you:: .hhh spoken privately
43          to any, e::r union leaders en and expressed
44          your view to them on a personal level would you
45          say.
46    IE:   Well what I say in public, and in private, tuh
47          evrybody involved in this, is, .h get round the
48          negotiating table, put aside the rhetoric and
49          stop this kind of thing happening again. .h These
50          strikes are wrong because negotiations er still
51          going on:, .h but parents en the public ev been
52          let dow:n, .h by- the government as we:ll, who've
53          acted in a reckless an' provocative manner.
54    IR:   .h=erm, You're a parent I'm a parent, lotta
55          people watching this will be parents, .hh erm
56          has it affected you personally this action='as
57          it- affected- your family an' friends I mean an'
58          and, .h what is the net effect of that gonna be
59          on, on parents, having t' take a day off work
60          today.
```

```
61   IE:   I think parents, up an' down the country've
62         been affected by this action. .h a-an' it's
63         wro:ng at a time when negotiations er still,
64         going on. (0.2) .h Parents've been let down
65         by both sides because the government has acted
66         in a reckless an' provocative manner. .hh I
67         think that both sides should after today's
68         disruption get round the negotiating table,
69         put aside the rhetoric, and stop this kinda
70         thing happening again.
```
(Interview ends)

As Ekström and Fitzgerald (2014) point out, repetition is a strategy used by both interviewers and interviewees for different purposes. They distinguish between "embedded" repetition in which the wording of a question or answer can be changed but a key phrase is nevertheless repeated, and "stripped" repetition in which the whole turn consists of a repeat, either word for word (as in an IR asking the same question over again—see chapter 5) or in slightly reordered form (as in Miliband's answers above). Thus, although Miliband here engages in "stripped" repetition, it is nonetheless possible to see that he makes some attempt to vary his answers: first of all by changing the order in which he repeats the four statements, and secondly by using prefaces that link the start of each of his answers to some aspect of the preceding question. For example, in extract (6) above, the IR's "have you spoken *privately*" (line 42) is linked via the phrase "what I say in public, and in *private*" (line 46), while "You're a *parent* I'm a *parent*" (line 54) is linked via the phrase "*parents*, up an' down the country've been affected" (line 61).

Despite this, media commentary rapidly fixed its attention on the sense of Miliband answering, "a series of different questions . . . by reciting a single soundbite over and over, like a mantra" (Brooker, 2011; see also Robinson, 2011), treating this as evidence of the vacuousness of political discourse in an age of media spin. Yet as Brooker (2011) acknowledges, a significant feature of this interview not so far mentioned is that it was not intended for broadcast on live television, but was recorded for distribution as a "pool" interview available to all news channels for their bulletins (cf. Ekström and Fitzgerald, 2014: 92–94). In that context, there is a sense in which Miliband's form of communication is a rational strategy. Communications managers know that the interview will be edited down before broadcast (Kroon-Lundell and Ekström 2010); hence, if they can ensure that all that the politician says on the tape is the intended soundbite, there is some guarantee that the necessary statement will, ultimately, find its way onto the broadcast news.

What is less common, however, is for whole, unedited versions of these pool interviews to appear in the public sphere. This is what happened in the Miliband case. In fact, for a long time after the event, the interview as transcribed above was accessible in its entirety on the BBC News website; at the time of writing it can still be found on YouTube. This leads to the second point of note, namely that this was the first of what became, for a time, a series of repetition-gaffe soundbite interviews to "go viral" in the social media.

A significant part of the reason for this is that the journalist who conducted the interview subsequently posted on his own blog a detailed account, not only of how the interview had been set up and managed by Miliband's political communications managers (including their need to be in control of the particular backdrop against which Mr. Miliband was filmed, with family photos visible over his left shoulder), but of his personal recollections of and reactions to what he clearly considers to have been the unacceptable behavior of his interviewee. As he writes,

> If news reporters and cameras are only there to be used by politicians as recording devices for their scripted soundbites, at best that is a professional discourtesy. At worst, if we are not allowed to explore and examine a politician's views, then politicians cease to be accountable in the most obvious way. So the fact that the unedited interview has found its way onto YouTube in all its absurdity, to be laughed at along with all the clips of cats falling off sofas, is perfectly proper. (Green, 2011: 1)

As in the previous two examples, significant media coverage—primarily in the press and on the internet—followed the posting of this blog and the YouTube video, as what was called the "Milibot" gaffe unfolded into the public sphere (Milibot of course being an amalgam of Mr. Miliband's name and the word "robot"). The significant feature here, of course, is that the journalist has taken advantage of the proliferation of communications channels within the contemporary media environment to feed that process with his own views on the professional discourtesy and lack of accountability that can emerge from political attempts to manage the conditions of total mediatization.

TOTAL MEDIATIZATION, MEDIA MANAGEMENT AND MEDIA ETHICS

The gaffe reveals something about the exquisite ambivalence of mediatized politics. This is perhaps why gaffes are so readily satirized in television comedies such as *Yes Minister*, *Veep* and *The Thick of It*. The attempts of political communications managers to control the process of mediatization by ensuring that politicians remain "on message" can themselves lead to a loss of control, as not only interviewers, but other journalists working for other media outlets, and indeed ordinary Twitter users and so on are scrutinizing their statements for mistakes that can be turned into reportable phenomena. Political cautiousness not only leads to perceptions of evasiveness or refusing to answer a "straight question"; infelicitous talk can itself be constituted by the remediation of things said within earshot of the rapidly inflating public sphere.

Thus, broadcast political interviews are two things simultaneously: (a) routine media events, for politicians, their communications advisers and for broadcast journalists; and (b) potentially explosive media phenomena. As all three examples above have demonstrated, in different ways, the broadcast political interview is at the heart of a discourse ecology, entwined with a whole range of mediation channels and associated means of public participation in the definition and redefinition of events.

We have seen how tiny lapses in the constant attention that is nowadays required by politicians and their advisers can reveal just how totally mediatized modern politics is. We have also seen how increasing diversification of mediated sources opens the possibility of a mutual entwinement of discourses that can rapidly spiral the definition, meanings and consequences of mundane events out of the grasp of even the most cautious political managers.

There is a form of media power involved here that also raises questions about journalistic responsibility and ethical conduct. In recent years there have been major public inquiries into the ethics of journalistic practice in the UK (the Leveson Inquiry) and elsewhere. The Leveson Inquiry was sparked by claims about press journalists illegally using technology to tap into the mobile phone messaging systems of people about whom they were writing stories, including, in one case, a kidnapped teenage girl. The inquiry resulted in the closure of a major British newspaper, the *News of the World*, and the jailing of a number of both editors and journalists.

Although the examples discussed in this chapter are far less consequential than some of the behavior revealed by Leveson, they do raise similar questions around the leaky boundaries between public and private in conditions of total mediatization; and the ways this leakiness might be utilized for the purposes of journalistic coups. Mullaney (2011), for example, cites the blog of the radio producer in the Gordon Brown case, who writes of the tape which Vine describes someone "handing" to him during his interview as "a dream spot—the Prime Minister revealing a chink in his carefully choreographed election campaign. Caught on tape—and seen by me before anyone else" (Hoffman, cited in Mullaney, 2011: 156). The prime minister himself also referred to the ethical dimension of this issue in his interview, immediately after the tape had been broadcast (extract 2, lines 54–59).

The leaks of off-record conversations, or posting of entire recordings of interviews not intended to be broadcast as such, that caused the embarrassments outlined above are sometimes justified using what in Atkinson and Silverman's (1997) terms would be an "interview society" rationale. As noted in chapter 1, they argue that there is a tendency to "celebrate the interview and the narrative data it produces as an especially authentic mode of social representation" (1997: 312). For example, Green's (2011) comments regarding the Miliband interview indicate that he believes Miliband's conduct to have revealed something authentic about politicians, namely that they are, in fact, inauthentic. This is also the gist of Brooker's (2011) commentary on that particular gaffe (see also, for a slightly different angle, Corner et al., 2013).

Here again we encounter the ambivalence of mediatization. Miliband and his advisers clearly understood the journalist's purpose in this case to be the production of a pool interview intended for subsequent editing, not a live broadcast or even an interview to appear "whole" in the public sphere. The interviewer, in his blog, invokes the professional ethics and responsibilities of journalism in contrast to the "professional discourtesy" exhibited by the politician. Yet at the same time, the interview having been placed, by someone, in its raw form on YouTube and the BBC News website, the celebration of the interview's laughability, in its new placement alongside "all the clips of cats falling off sofas," is only from one perspective "perfectly proper." From another, it is ethically questionable.

Although the landscape of mediatization is expanding and evolving, therefore, the broadcast interview remains a highly significant social and cultural phenomenon. The changing technologies of media and communication, and their affordances, do not lessen its importance as a form of political discourse. If anything, they increase it.

Chapter Four

Rules of Engagement
The Conventional Political Interview

Interviews are, of course, occasions of talk: talk-in-interaction between professional journalists and political actors of various sorts. We have now seen some examples of how that talk itself is potentially consequential within the wider media ecology. In this chapter, we begin to consider in more detail how interviews are formed as distinctive theaters of action, outlining the "rules of engagement" that the actors within them use to structure their actions. The main focus here will be on the workaday or conventional political interview, before moving on in subsequent chapters to more adversarial, aggressive, and hybrid interview types.

THE CONVENTIONAL POLITICAL INTERVIEW

In chapter 1, I distinguished between workaday and spotlight political interviews, pointing out that while the latter can often draw public attention because of the detailed probing open to the interviewer, the former are far more commonplace in everyday news broadcasting. In this chapter my aim is to show that the basic turn-taking structures of the news interview can be derived from more or less any selected example of a workaday interview; and that it is these structures that underpin the more adversarial, aggressive and hybrid interview formats that I consider in future chapters. In such an interview, which I refer to as the *conventional political interview* (CPI), the interviewer's task is not approached in a particularly adversarial or otherwise challenging way (we come to that in the next chapter), but mainly as an attempt to coax further information about a specific topic from an interviewee with knowledge, experience or expertise relevant to the matter at hand.

We can think of this format as conventional in two related senses. First, it is based on a fairly restricted set of *turn-taking conventions*, as suggested above and further illustrated below. Second, interviews most closely conducted according to those turn-taking conventions tend to come across, in the normative sense, as a *conventional type* of broadcast interview; that is, routine, uncontroversial, nothing special, and so on.

I use a recently recorded example of an interview utilizing this conventional interview modality to illustrate the key features. The interview was selected from a randomly chosen episode of the BBC's flagship news program *Today*. The interview concerns the fairly mundane question of inflation rates, consumer behavior and banking policy.

The standard way in which daily news programs such as *Today* are organized is in terms of a series of interviews in which the interviewer role is distributed among a team of four or five journalists, with one of the team usually also acting as an anchor: that is, providing short continuity announcements between interviews, introducing each item, handing over to the assigned interviewer, and accepting a hand-back from the interviewer at the end of each interview. The show is three hours long and each episode contains an average of fifteen items (plus hourly news bulletins). Most items run for between five and ten minutes; interviews with major figures are allocated a longer slot of fifteen to twenty minutes. In one or two cases, interviews may be repeated: for example, an interview first broadcast early in the morning may appear again toward the end of the show.

In the following transcript of a short, three-minute interview, AN represents the anchor, while as elsewhere in the book, IR represents the interviewer and IE the interviewee. I will first present the interview in its entirety, transcribed according to the standard CA method, before later taking certain segments from it to illustrate standard turn-taking conventions of the interview.

```
(1) R4: Jack-Julius

1    AN:    It's a quarter past seven.=Inflation::, is low very
2           low. In fact prices could be heading down. Simon Jack
3           c'n ex[plain.
4    IR:         [.mhhh (.) Thanks Michelle=Yes inflation in
5           December wuz nought point five per cent in January,
6           it was nought point three, see what I'm doing here
7           today we're gunna get the reading fuh February,
8           some say it could be zero or e:ven, u-negative.
```

```
9            .hhhh Er this is partly because of falling oil
10           and food prices=.h=the key question the int'resting
11           thing is, .h how do we beha::ve, in the face of
12           falling prices if that's what we get, .h=an' what
13           should the Bank uv ↑England do. Deanne Julius, is
14           an economist, and founder member of the bank's,
15           .h monet'ry policy committee=>en is in our radio
16           car<=Good mornin:g,
17    IE:    .hhth (.) Good morning.=
18    IR:    =.hhh S- what is:- i-if it is zero or below what're
19           the implications uh that.
20           (0.5)
21    IE:    .hthh Well I think the implications ar:e that uh
22           people will be spending less money, o:n food an'
23           fuel, and have more money duh spend on other
24           things. .hhh Thee er, .hh as you rightly say
25           thee-the key issue is w- why is it low why is it
26           falling, .hh an:d, (.) I think in the case uv
27           Britain at least it's <falling becau:se u::v,> s-
28           things that happened on the supply si:de,
29           u-erw- specially to oil prices, .hhh not
30           because we have a particu'ly weak, demand side.
31    IR:    So this is good deflation in the sense that it
32           puts more money in our pockets rather than
33           the- ba:d deflation where we think oh if things
34           er gunna get cheaper maybe I'll, hh defe:r my
35           purchases I'll buy something next month or next
36           year.
37           (0.9)
38    IE:    .hhhh I think given the strength of the- British
```

```
39            economy the job market an' so forth this is almost
40            certainly: good:. (.) deflation, .hh but it's::
41            it's also, temporary. (.) h deflation. .hh
42            Remember it may not actually be deflation but
43            what some people call lowflation, .hhh meaning
44            e:u:er:: plus or minus one percent but aro:und
45            stable prices. .hh So thee:- u- th-the key thing
46            is that it's happened because of some big oil
47            price an' food price fa:lls, .hh those won't
48            last for ever they'll fall out uv the index, er .hh
49            in the way c- inflation's calculated so, I would
50            say in three or four month's ti:me, we'll
51            prob'ly be back up to:, one and a half:,
52            somewhere near two percent.
53    IR:     Now you've sat in that meeting of the ni:ne M P C:,
54            members.=N-Andy Haldane who's the current chief
55            economist, .hh said in a speech last week that
56            he wuz beginning tuh think w- 'e said it was a
57            personal view .hh that the risk i:s that in fact
58            no:w, h we may not see inflation bounce back an'
59            be at the two percent target over time an' th't
60            the risks er >all the downside<=.hhh his bo:ss Mark
61            Carney, said to lower rates would be lunacy
62            right now, wha-what's it like being in that
63            room.
64            (0.3)
65    IE:     .mthhh Well it sounds like it's more exciting
66            now than it's been fer a coupla years when they
67            haven't moved int're(h)st r(h)ates at a:ll .hhhh
68            E::r eu-y- I think it- it's- it's a good thing
```

```
69            that- Andy and people like him, ar::e challenging
70            thee, thee received wisdom, .hhh but I'm su:re
71            Andy himself would e:ur, would admit that- nobody
72            really knows what direction it's going to go:
73            an' it'll depend a lot on what happens in the
74            Eurozo:ne and .hh and er with Opec. So um:: the
75            the bank needs tuh be- .hhh be vigilant about
76            those things, but just as it did no:t, e:rw
77            change int'rest rates when intr- when: inflation
78            went .hh far above target, a few years ago,
79            .hh I think it's pretty unlikely to: e:r to
80            overreact, and er move int'rest rates certainly
81            not dow:n, in the next, coupla months.
82            (0.2)
83     IR:    E- f- Deanne Julius, thank you very much, i:ndeed,
84            er we've >just got a little piece of news< that
85            uh, .h a group has launched a multi billion pound
86            law suit against Tesco in the U K, .h becoz of
87            thee price-=u-thee, accounting crisis which saw
88            that black ho:le, materially affect their share
89            price=they say they want t'claim some of that
90            back=have more of that later.=
91     AN:    =.h Simon thank you
       ((END))
```

Although, at 91 lines, the transcript seems quite long, in fact, as noted above, the interview takes up only three minutes of airtime. Within that three minutes, the overall structure of the interview takes a standard shape, which can be fairly simply described.

It begins with a brief contextualizing statement, or "lead-in," from the anchor, who then names the interviewer as a way of handing over the item to him:

```
(1) Detail

1    AN:      It's a quarter past seven.=Inflation::, is low very
2             low. In fact prices could be heading down. Simon Jack
3             c'n ex[plain.
```

The interviewer acknowledges the hand-over, naming the anchor in turn (line 4). In fact, he can be heard initiating his turn to speak just before the anchor finishes her turn, with his in-breath (".mhhh"). This slight overlap might be seen as a way of ensuring close coordination between the two speakers. But in fact, it turns out to be mildly disruptive, as the IR then waits for a tiny pause (the (.) in the transcript) to make sure that AN's handover ("'Simon Jack c'n explain'") is in fact complete.

```
(1) Detail

2             low. In fact prices could be heading down. Simon Jack
3             c'n ex[plain.
4→   IR:      [.mhhh (.) Thanks Michelle
```

The reason for this minor disfluency may derive from the slightly unconventional wording in the AN's handover: "Simon Jack c'n explain," as opposed to the more conventional "Simon Jack has that story," or "Simon Jack is with economist Deanne Julius."

Following this handover, IR quickly shifts his address toward the overhearing audience (the = sign indicates a rush-through or latching effect) and produces his own, more detailed introductory statement (lines 4–13).

```
(1) Detail

4    IR:      [.mhhh (.) Thanks Michelle=Yes inflation in
5             December wuz nought point five per cent in January,
6             it was nought point three, see what I'm doing here
7             today we're gunna get the reading fuh February,...
```

Next, he introduces the upcoming interviewee by naming her, stating her expertise in relation to the news item ("an economist"), indicating for listeners that she is in a remote location ("our radio car"), and initiating a greetings exchange (lines 16–17):

```
(1) Detail

13    IR:    ........Deanne Julius, is
14           an economist, and founder member of the bank's,
15           .h monet'ry policy committee=>en is in our radio
16           car<=Good mornin:g,
17    IE:    .hhth (.) Good morning.
```

The bulk of the interview then consists of an exchange of questions and answers on the designated topic (lines 18–81). It is here that the crucial work of "interviewing" is done; and we will return to dissect this long section later in the chapter.

Finally, the IR thanks the IE (line 83) and at this point the interview itself is over. However, in handing back to the AN, IR in this case mentions some related news that is just coming in and promises further reports later in the program (lines 84–90). The hand-over is completed by the AN thanking the IR, again by name (line 91).

One thing that is demonstrated here is the means by which interviews on news programs such as this are situated within a "news flow" consisting of the set of items deemed newsworthy on that day by the editors and producers. Each news item takes a similar trajectory, passing from anchor to interviewer to interviewee, back to interviewer and thence to anchor; with in this particular case an added illustration of the unfolding nature of the news as preliminaries for further items to appear later are tagged onto the end of the interview itself.

However, looking more closely at the design and sequential organization of the utterances that make up the body of this interview allows us to reveal much more about the conventions of the news interview as an interactionally accomplished form of institutional talk.

The news interview is characterized by two main turn-taking structures: *question-answer-next question* and *question-answer-formulation*. Both of these structures, as we will see, are present in the interview reproduced as extract (1). Both structures are crucial to the way in which journalists in broadcast news orient to their professional role. News interviewers may act as questioners, but they also see it as their role to present a balanced account of events while avoiding taking up positions which can be heard as partial, either on their own part or in their capacity as representatives of news organizations. In many cases, this requirement for balance is written into the licensing agreements of news channels, particularly those, such as the BBC, with a public service remit.

In analyzing these sequential structures and speech practices, we can come to see how the turn-taking system of the interview is uniquely adapted to the constraints and requirements of journalistic objectivity.

QUESTION-ANSWER-NEXT QUESTION

In many types of question-answer sequence, in ordinary conversation as well as institutional settings such as classroom teaching, there occurs a third position slot in which the questioner acknowledges or evaluates the answer. Thus, in conversational information-seeking questions, we may find a question-answer-acknowledgement sequence, as in the following example:

```
(2)  (Button and Casey, 1985: 21) ((From ordinary conversation))
1    Clara:   How's yer foot?
2    Agnes:   Oh it's healing beautif'lly!
3→   Clara:   Goo::d.
```

Having asked the question in line 1 that occasions the positive answer in line 2, Clara goes on to acknowledge the "good news" about Agnes's healing foot in line 3.

Similarly, in the kind of knowledge-testing questions asked by classroom teachers we often find a three-part question-answer-evaluation sequence, as in:

```
(3)  (Coulthard, 1977: 100) ((From classroom interaction))
1    Teacher:  Can you tell me why do you eat all that food.
2              Yes.
3    Pupil:    To keep you strong.
4→   Teacher:  To keep you strong. Yes. To keep you strong.
```

Here, in line 4, the teacher repeats the answer proffered by the pupil, evaluates it ("Yes"), then repeats it again, as a way of demonstrating to the class its correctness.

In news interviews, by contrast, there is generally no third-turn acknowledgement or evaluation. As we can see in this detail from extract (1), once the IR judges that the IE's answer to his preceding question is complete, he moves straight into the *next* question:

```
(1) Detail

49   IE:   in the way c- inflation's calculated so, I would
50         say in three or four month's ti:me, we'll
51         prob'ly be back up to:, one and a half:,
52         somewhere near two percent.
53→  IR:   Now you've sat in that meeting of the ni:ne M P C:,
54         members.=N-Andy Haldane who's the current chief
55         economist, .hh said in a speech last week that
```

In line 53, the IR could begin his new turn with an intermediate action which relates back to the preceding answer: an acknowledgement or evaluation such as, "Ok that's great. Now you've sat in that meeting..." Instead, the IR simply embarks on a new topic, launching straight into a next question: "Now you've sat in that meeting of the ni:ne M P C: members..."

The general avoidance of third-position acknowledgements and evaluations acts as one of a number of noteworthy features of the question-answer chaining sequence that is specific to news interviews. By withholding acknowledgements and evaluations, interviewers in the conventional modality avoid taking up positions on the talk produced in interviewees' answers. They thereby act as conduits facilitating the interviewee's talk and maintaining a sense in which that talk is produced, primarily, not for the interviewer but for the audience. As we will see in later chapters, there are other interview modalities in which these practices are less in evidence, and this changes the nature of the journalist's role considerably.

In the conventional modality, it is also the case that interviewers routinely and systematically minimize their use of the kind of continuers, receipt tokens and newsmarkers (such as "uh huh," "right," "yeah," "oh really?" and so on) that are regularly found in ordinary conversational turn-taking. In ordinary interaction, such items do the work of situating their producer as the intended, and attentive, primary recipient of the talk being produced by an interlocutor (Schegloff, 1982). Hence, by withholding their production, news interviewers again effectively preserve a sense in which it is the audience, rather than themselves, who are the primary recipients of the interviewee's talk.

Therefore, such practices are bound up with the means by which the talk is produced as broadcast talk—that is, specifically for the benefit of an overhearing audience. The withholding of acknowledgements, evaluations and continuers is significant for two main reasons:

First, their production would identify prior talk as news for questioners (who are usually fully briefed beforehand or may be required to appear so) rather than the overhearing audience . . . for whom it is, putatively, news. Second, by their production of these receipt objects . . . questioners identify themselves as the primary recipients of the talk they elicit [and] audiences could . . . come to view themselves as literally the overhearers of colloquies that, rather than being produced for them, were being produced and treated as private. (Heritage, 1985:100)

However, none of this means, even in the conventional modality, that interviewers do not actually possess opinions, or that they do not sometimes find ways of inflecting their questions so as to evaluate an interviewee's response or convey a particular stance on an issue or on the conduct of an interviewee's talk on the issue. Apart from the question-answer-next question sequence, our illustrative interview in extract (1) contains examples of the two principal practices by which interviewers can do this while remaining formally neutral: the question-answer-formulation sequence, and the footing shift.

NEUTRALISM AND FOOTING

One of the key aspects of news journalism is the focus on "objective" questioning. In their role as questioners, interviewers are required to avoid stating their views or opinions on the news. Rather, their task is to elicit the stance, opinion or account of the one being questioned, but to do so at least technically without bias or prejudice. This is bound up with the professional journalistic ethos of neutrality, in which journalists (including broadcast journalists) are seen as acting in the interests of a wider public in extracting information from individuals in the news. Clayman (1988) argues that instead of neutrality, we should prefer the term "neutralism" in discussions of news interview talk. While "neutrality" implies that the interviewer is, in fact, some kind of a neutral conduit putting questions merely to extract information from interviewees (an interpretation often favored by news professionals themselves), "neutralism" foregrounds the fact that news interviewers actively achieve the status of "being neutral" through a set of specialized discourse practices.

One such practice is the "footing shift." Goffman (1981) developed the concept of footing to describe the varying ways in which speakers in ordinary conversation are able to take up positions of proximity or distance with respect to the sentiments expressed in an utterance. Distinguishing between the *animator* (the producer of the utterance), the *author* (the person whose words are actually being uttered) and the *principal* (the person whose viewpoint, stance, belief, etcetera, the utterance expresses), Goffman noted that at any moment in talk, the animator can exhibit differing degrees of authorship and principalship regarding the words he or she is speaking.

For example, in the following extract from ordinary conversation, one speaker (Ginny) adopts three different footings in a short space of time while discussing with her friend how often she and her boyfriend should meet up:

```
(4)  (Clayman, 1992: 163-4) ((From ordinary conversation))

1→   Ginny:   We don't wanna see one another, (.) .hh on a
2             weekend where we just have (.) y'know two
3             days if [even tha]:t.
4    Sarah:           [ Right. ]
5             (.)
6    Sarah:   tch I [don't blame you.]
7    Ginny:         [tuh relate tuh o]ne another. .hh Y'know
8             we'd like- (.) a little bit longer than tha:t.
9             (0.2)
10   Sarah:   Right.=
11→  Ginny:   =I mean I don't (.) really care that much.
12→           But he does.
```

In lines 1–3, and again in lines 7–8, Ginny adopts a footing in which she is *animator* and *author* of her speech (that is, she is not purporting to quote words "authored" by someone else); yet she is recruiting her boyfriend as a joint *principal* of the sentiment expressed—it is a feeling shared by both of them. Later, in lines 11 and 12, she separates out this joint principalship such that, in 11, she acts as sole principal expressing her own feelings, while in 12, she attributes authorship of a different feeling to her boyfriend, thus shifting footing to recruit him as a third-party principal.

Broadcast news interviewers often use footing shifts in order to give the appearance of formal neutrality (Clayman, 1992). Consider the following example:

```
(5)  NBC: Kalb-Dole

1→   IR:   It is s::aid that ((the president's)) programs are
2          in trouble,though he seems to be terribly popular
3          with the American people.
```

```
    4               (0.6)
    6→              It is said by some people at thuh White House
    7               we could get those programs through if only we
    8               ha:d perhaps more: .hh effective leadership
    9               on on thuh hill an' I [suppose] indirectly=
   10    IE:                             [hhhheh  ]
   11    IR:        =that might (0.5) relate t'you as well:. (0.6)
   12               Uh what d'you think thuh problem is really.
   13→              is=it (0.2) thuh leadership as it might be
   14               claimed up on thuh hill, er is it thuh
   15               programs themselves.
```

In this question the interviewer seeks to highlight challenges to the effectiveness of the president's programs and his leadership. We can note that in at least two places, the IR shifts footing so that he is no longer author of the sentiments expressed, and principalship becomes ambivalent: first, "It is s::aid" in line 3, and second, "It is said by some people at thuh White House" in line 6. In other words, in constructing this challenging question for the IE, while the IR remains animator of the words, he *redistributes authorship* for the position that lies behind his eventual question, and this in turn renders principalship at least somewhat ambivalent: the IR is putting the question, but he is using the views of others to back it up, thereby retaining his own stance of neutralism.

A further feature illustrated here is the use of a *question-preface* in allowing the IR to address controversial issues and construct challenging questions. In the question-answer turn-taking system of the news interview, interviewers are permitted to produce turns formatted grammatically as statements, rather than questions, in only very specific circumstances. The principal convention of neutralism that relates to the use of statements by interviewers is this:

1. Interviewers may use statements but only in the framework of putting a question (i.e., as question-prefaces)
2. Interviewees should refrain from speaking until a question has been asked (i.e., treat statements as prefatory to questions)

In the extract above we see the IR making a series of statements, prefatory to the question he puts in lines 12–15. Note that even when the question gets asked, after the statement-formulated preface, the footing shift is sustained:

"is=it (0.2) the leadership *as it might be claimed* up on the hill . . ." (lines 13–14).

The next extract shows how interviewers may initiate repair on their turns in order to insert a footing shift which turns the utterance from one in which they begin by expressing an opinion, to one where that opinion is attributed to others.

```
(6)  AMS: Marr-McDonnell

1      IE:   I'm hoping as well by the way, that Dawn Butler
2            gets on the ballot paper too=I think it would be
3            really good, .h tuh have Dawn's voice there=a
4            black woman, .hh representi::ng er a section of
5            the party as well. .h Let's give the members
6            a choice.
7→     IR:   Su-=It does sound a little bit, er w- what would
8→           you say tuh people who say this sounds a little
9            bit, .h as if it is more important, .h fuh the
10           left, tuh keep control of the party, tha:n to
11           get the very best people who can get you back
12           into power in due course.
```

Having begun, in line 7, to ask a question the wording of which heavily implies that he will be both author and principal of the view behind the question ("It does sound a little bit..."), the interviewer breaks off and then initiates self-repair in order, once again, to redistribute authorship, "what would you say tuh *people who say* this sounds a little bit . . ."

The illustrative interview reproduced in extract (1) contains an example of this kind of practice. The interviewer's use of a turn containing footing shifts can be seen in lines 53–62:

```
(1)  Detail

53     IR:   Now you've sat in that meeting of the ni:ne M P C:,
54→          members.=N-Andy Haldane who's the current chief
55           economist, .hh said in a speech last week that
56→          he wuz beginning tuh think w- 'e said it was a
```

```
57          personal view .hh that the risk i:s that in fact
58          no:w, h we may not see inflation bounce back an'
59          be at the two percent target over time an' th't
60          the risks er >all the downside<=.hhh his bo:ss Mark
61→         Carney, said to lower rates would be lunacy
62          right now, wha-what's it like being in that
63          room.
64          (0.3)
65   IE:    .mthhh Well it sounds like it's more exciting
66          now than it's been fer a coupla years when they
67          haven't moved int're(h)st r(h)ates at a:ll
```

Due to this interview's non-combative modality, this example does not show the interviewer using shifts in footing to challenge the interviewee. Rather, he uses positions attributed to third parties, which are themselves potentially different takes on the issue, to pose a fairly cooperative question inviting the interviewee to describe from her experience the atmosphere in which monetary policy committee meetings are held. This may be informative, for the audience; however, it is certainly not a challenging or probing question.

The primary significance of footing shifts is that their use enables the interviewer to fulfill two professional tasks simultaneously: to be formally neutral, while offering challenges or alternative perspectives to the views stated by interviewees. Interviewers routinely use footing shifts when they want to put forward alternative viewpoints for discussion, to counter an interviewee and put the other side of an argument. If they did this while retaining a combined footing of animator, author and principal, they would inevitably be heard as taking up positions in their own right (as is almost the case in extract 6, line 10). With the footing shift, they can avoid this and achieve at least a hearable approximation of impartiality.

FORMULATIONS

Another technique for producing talk that is critical and challenging toward interviewees, and which is also bound up with the production of talk for an overhearing audience, is that of "formulating" the gist or upshot of the interviewee's remarks, usually in pursuit of some controversial or newsworthy aspect. Formulating involves a speaker "summarizing, glossing, or developing the gist of an informant's earlier statements" (Heritage, 1985: 100). It tends to be an activity undertaken by questioners in institutional settings, such as medical professionals, or as we will see below, news interviewers.

There are at least two aspects to why formulations are so frequently utilized by interviewers. One is that the practice of summarizing or glossing can act as a means of packaging or repackaging the central point made in an interviewee's turn for the benefit of the overhearing audience. The other is that the same practice can also be used to construct a stronger or more contentious version of the interviewee's stated position. In this, the interviewer can be seen to be challenging the interviewee but, once again, without overtly taking up a position in his or her own right.

Extract (7) shows an example of a more cooperative type of formulation:

```
(7) WAO: Common Agricultural Policy

1     IE:    I'm all for having a common agricultural policy, (0.6)
2            but I think it's absurd to suggest that decisions of
3            (.) immense economic magnitude .hhh should be taken
4            enti:rely by .hh (.) the ministers who are (.) most
5            int'rested in one particular segment of the
6            community.=I wouldn't want Ministers d-Defence
7            to take all the decisions on defence and I wouldn't
8            want Ministers of .hhhh of Education to take all
9            the decisions on education.=
10→   IR:    =.hhh So you're suggesting there that the farm
11           ministers shouldn't decide all this entirely amongst
12           themselves that it should be .hhh spread across
13           the board amongst all ministers.
14    IE:    Exactly.=I'm saying that one must find some way
15           of (.) of bringing other responsibilities (.)
16           particularly those representing the tax payer
17           and the consumer as well as the farmer .hhh much
18           more into the picture.
```

In line 10, the interviewer produces a turn which formulates the interviewee's immediately prior answer. The formulation is "cooperative" in the sense that it seeks to clarify the viewpoint expressed in the answer, possibly for the benefit of the overhearing audience. For instance, in lines 1–9 the IE has given a slightly convoluted answer framed largely in terms of what he "wouldn't want" to see. The IR's formulation restates that view in terms of what the IE seems to be arguing *should* happen rather than what should not: that decisions on agricultural policy should be "spread across the board amongst all ministers."

Again, there is an example of the formulation sequence in the interview reproduced in extract (1). It occurs in the turn beginning at line 31:

```
(1) Detail
 24    IE:   .... .hhh Thee er, .hh as you rightly say
 25          thee-the key issue is w- why is it low why is it
 26          falling, .hh an:d, (.) I think in the case uv
 27          Britain at least it's <falling becau:se u::v,> s-
 28          things that happened on the supply si:de,
 29          u-erw- specially to oil prices, .hhh not
 30          because we have a particu'ly weak, demand side.
 31→   IR:   So this is good deflation in the sense that it
 32          puts more money in our pockets rather than
 33          the- ba:d deflation where we think oh if things
 34          er gunna get cheaper maybe I'll, hh defe:r my
 35          purchases I'll buy something next month or next
 36          year.
 37          (0.9)
 38    IE:   .hhhh I think given the strength of the- British
 39          economy the job market an' so forth this is almost
 40          certainly: good:. (.) deflation, .hh but it's::
 41          it's also, temporary. (.) h deflation.
```

Once more, in line with the general tenor of this interview, the interviewer uses the formulation cooperatively. His turn begins, as do most formulations, with an upshot-marker, "So," and then goes on to offer a summary of what he understands the interviewee to be saying in response to his earlier question ("this is good deflation . . . rather than ba:d deflation . . . ").

Rules of Engagement 67

As in extract (7), the version presented here is noticeably simplified. It is also audience-oriented, in the sense that it refers to mundane issues such as "money in our p<u>o</u>ckets" and the price of things in the shops rather than, as in the IE's previous turn, potentially esoteric matters such as "things that happened on the supp<u>ly</u> si:de" (line 28).

A central sequential feature of formulations is that they make relevant in the next turn a response in which a recipient either agrees or disagrees with the version being put forward. In the above cases, the IE agrees with the IR's version, in the detail from (1) even adopting his phrase in "this is almost certainly: g<u>oo</u>d:. (.) deflation . . . "

Formulations can also be used not only to simplify, but also to upgrade and, at least implicitly, criticize the interviewee's remarks. The following extract provides two illustrations of this:

```
(8) TVN: Tea

1     IE:   What in fact happened was that in the course of last
2           year, .hh the price went up really very sharply, .hhh
3           and uh the blenders did take advantage of this: uh
4           to obviously to raise their prices to retailers. (0.7)
5           .hhh They haven't been so quick in reducing their
6           prices when the world market prices come down. (0.3)
7           .hh And so this means that price in the sh- the
8           prices in the shops have stayed up .hh really rather
9           higher than we'd like to see them.
10          (0.7)
11→   IR:   So you- you're really accusing them of profiteering.
12    IE:   .hhh No they're in business to make money that's
13          perfectly sensible.=We're also saying that uh: .hh
14          it's not a trade which is competitive as we would
15          like it.=There're four (0.2) blenders which have
16          together eighty five percent of the market .hhh
17          and uh we're not saying that they (.) move in
18          concert or anything like that but we'd like the
19          trade to be a bit more competitive.=
```

```
20→  IR:   =But you're giving them: a heavy instruction (.) as
21         it were to (.) to reduce their prices.
22   IE:   .hh What we're saying is we think that prices
23         could come down without the blenders losing their
24         profit margins
```

The interviewee here is the chairman of trading regulator the Price Commission, who is being interviewed about the Commission's report on tea prices. Looking at the two arrowed IR turns (lines 11 and 20), what we find is an emergent dispute over what IE can be taken as "really saying." In line 11, for instance, the interviewer formulates the long turn in lines 1–9 as "really accusing [the blenders] of profiteering." Since the interviewee had not himself used the term "profiteering," this formulation can be described as inferentially elaborating a claim proposed to be implicit in IE's remarks.

As noted, formulations make relevant in the next turn a response in which a recipient either agrees or disagrees with the version being put forward. In this case, IE disagrees with the "profiteering" formulation (line 12) and quickly moves on to address another issue, lack of competitiveness. In line 20, the interviewer comes back in to formulate these remarks, again using much stronger terms than the interviewee; and once again (in lines 22–24), IE puts forward a weaker version of his argument than the "heavy instruction . . . to reduce prices" referred to in the formulation.

We thus find a form of dispute in which, while not taking up a position in his own right (and therefore maintaining the professional journalistic stance of impartiality), the news interviewer nonetheless uses his ability to formulate the gist or upshot of the interviewee's remarks to attempt to unpack some underlying agenda proposedly at work in them.

Although Heritage (1985) suggests that formulations are neutral in the sense that they avoid commenting on or making assessments of the content of a prior turn, he also shows that formulations can "make something more of [a topic] than was originally presented in the . . . prior turn" (Heritage, 1985: 101). In fact, formulations are rarely entirely neutral. Rather, they act as candidate *re-presentations* of what an interlocutor can be taken as having said, or meant. Such candidate re-presentations are selective, in that they focus on a particular element of the prior talk and preserve that element as the topic for further talk.

The following two examples show how the inferentially elaborative probe-type formulation can be also used by IRs more contentiously, to present a specific position *on behalf of* an IE whose response to an initial question is hearable as somehow evasive.

Extract (9) shows an IR asking about a recently published set of proposed reforms to employment regulation by the Labour Party:

```
(9) Politics Live: Labour Policy
1    IR:   You run an organisation called Reform, (0.2) there
2          was loads of refor:ms here, which ones did you
3          like which ones did you hate.
4          (.)
5    IE:   So:, I thought that some of the diagnosis, of the
6          problems we're faci:ng was very good. Erm, .hh and,
7→   IR:   Oh, so you didn't like any of the reforms. Hm! h .h!
```

The IR's question is fairly open in that it invites the IE to select particular reforms and comment on them, either negatively or positively. However, rather than addressing the reforms, the IE begins her response by highlighting the party's "diagnosis, of the problems we're faci:ng" with which she agrees. This is interpreted by the IR as the first part in a contrastive pair, the second part of which would be to disagree with the reforms themselves. The formulation in line 7 makes this inference clear, proposing as the IE's position that she (therefore) "didn't like any of the reforms."

In extract (10), taken from an interview that is considered at greater length in chapter 5, the IR asks whether the IE, Home Secretary Michael Howard, is proposing that a high-ranking official in the prison service, Derek Lewis, is "lying" in his account of a controversial dispute between the two of them:

```
(10) Newsnight: Paxman-Howard
1    IR:   Derek Lewis says, Howard had certainly told me that
2          the governor of Parkhurst should be suspended, and
3          had threatened to overrule me. Are you saying
4          Mr Lewis is lying?=
5    IE:   =e-I have (.) given a full account of this, and the
6          position is, what I told the House of Commons=and
7          let me tell you what the po[sition is
8→   IR:                              [So you a:re saying
```

```
 9→               Mr Lewis [is ly[ing.
10    IE:                  [Le-   [Let me tell you what the position is.
```

Although the question is posed in straightforward polar (Yes/No) terms (lines 3–4), the IE manifestly declines to answer the question as stated, and refers back to the "ac<u>cou</u>nt" that he previously gave to a House of Commons select committee. In other words, he sticks to his own story about the dispute with Lewis. The IR's formulation, in lines 8–9, presents this sticking to the story as, in fact, a tacit admission that the answer to his original question ("<u>A</u>re you saying Mr. Lewis is <u>ly</u>ing?") must therefore be "Yes" —an accusation that, for a serving government minister, could prove to be highly damaging.

As extract (10) in particular shows, formulations can sometimes reveal an underlying agenda on their producer's part, which in turn can be cooperative, uncooperative or openly disputatious. The formulation opens a sequential slot in which the interlocutor may, in the next turn, accept, reject, or otherwise respond to the formulation. Or, as in extract (10), the IE may even ignore the formulation and attempt to proceed with his previous answer. Whatever the response, the formulation itself positions its producer less as a neutral conduit than an active interpreter of the preceding talk—while also, as has been noted, avoiding any explicit endorsement of a position in his or her own right.

Formulations are more common in forms of institutional interaction than in mundane conversation (Heritage, 1985: 100). But this is not just a matter of statistical frequency. In the examples discussed above, the ability to formulate is bound up with the institutional work being undertaken via the dialogue. In a news interview it is the interviewee's role to answer questions and challenges put to him or her by a professional interviewer, who acts on behalf of the general public interest but whose own view ideally plays no part in the exchange. Interviewees are therefore "on the line" in these exchanges: it is their views, opinions and answers which are at the heart of the talk. For this reason, interviewers are structurally positioned to elicit talk that is "on the record"—talk in which it is as clear as possible what the interviewee is "really saying." There is also the issue, of course, that interviewers are broadcasters, and may be systematically oriented to the importance of clarifying their interlocutor's talk for the benefit of the overhearing audience. Formulations, as candidate summaries, promptings, focusings, recyclings and the like, are particularly useful in the pursuit of these institutional aims.

CONCLUSION

In this chapter, I have outlined the most important aspects of the organization of interaction, and the corresponding interactional organization of news production, in the conventional political interview. I highlighted the role of the *question-answer-next question* turn-taking sequence in structuring the interview as a theater of language use. But this turn-taking pattern merely provides a framework within which a whole range of activities may be taking place. In the news interview context, those other activities include probing and challenging questioning, and drawing out agendas and implications from interviewees' answers. The key point that has been emphasized is the importance, in this, of *neutralism*—defined as the asking of questions that can be probing or challenging while retaining the appearance of neutrality. I then looked in some detail at the ways in which, within that constrained sequential structure, journalists have developed ways of using syntactic and grammatical forms such as the footing shift or the formulation to do the work of responsible questioning in ways that are adapted to the unique requirements of journalistic neutralism.

As we see in more detail in subsequent chapters, moving outside the interactionally managed conventions of neutralism threatens to call into question the very nature of the interactional event as an interview: simple shifts in turn-taking practices can begin to transform "interview" into "argument." Starting in chapter 5 with well-established *adversarial* and *accountability* interview practices, we go on in later chapters to look at the ways in which the basic set of interview conventions is modified, modulated and hybridized in more recent forms of broadcast political interview, as the interviewer's role—and, in many respects, the response of the interviewee—is cast in a more argumentative, and indeed emotional mold.

Chapter Five

"It's a Simple Question"
The Adversarial Political Interview

In their study of courtroom interaction in the adversarial legal system that operates in the UK and USA, Atkinson and Drew (1979) pointed out that while the examination and cross-examination of witnesses is organized at least formally according to a question-answer speech exchange system, that is only a minimal characterization of what is going on in individual turns. Any of a wide range of actions may be done in a given turn: mounting an accusation, imputing bad character, exhibiting skepticism, or defending against any of these actions. The proviso is that such actions should be done in the *form* of a question or an answer.

By now it should be clear that a similar thing may be said about the question-answer turn-taking system of the news interview. Even the most neutralistic interview is not necessarily a sterile occasion in which, purely and simply, questions get asked and answers given. Question prefaces, footing shifts and formulations, together with other interpretive strategies, can be used to do more with a turn than merely acting as a conduit for information gathering.

However, there are, and for many years have been, types of broadcast political interview that adopt much more explicitly the kind of adversarial questioning techniques that can be found in the courtroom. Here, interviews become interactional events in which journalists may seek much more overtly to challenge politicians and other public figures, and in which those public figures may, in turn, utilize strategies to resist such challenges. The interview thus becomes a domain of contestation, an interactional combat zone, in which broadcast journalists pursue one agenda while political actors make it their business to pursue quite another. In fact, the whole question of what "the question" is, along with what might constitute an "answer," typically becomes the very topic of interaction in these more adversarial forms of political interview.

I begin by looking at a rather extreme example of this dynamic, examining what can happen when an interviewer's attempt to construct an adversarial question in the first place is interrupted or "derailed" by interviewee talk.

DERAILING THE QUESTION

In a previous chapter, I showed an example of an interviewee moving outside the conventions of "being interviewed" and seeking instead to adopt the questioner role. In that example, the interviewer's response was an illustration of how those very conventions are actively policed by the participants themselves. Here, by way of contrast, I briefly discuss a historical example of what can happen when the interview conventions seem to break down completely, and the interaction appears to become less of an "interview" and more of a "confrontation" (something that gets far more attention in later chapters). What we will find in this particular case, using CA to examine an extract from the interview in detail, is that rather than breaking down, the conventions are in fact manipulated in pursuit of competing agendas, with the interviewee, perhaps knowingly, repeatedly seeking to derail the interviewer's attempt to construct an adversarial question.

The extract is from a famous 1988 interview between Dan Rather of CBS News and then Vice-President George Bush Sr. (see for further analysis of this case, Clayman and Whalen, 1989; Nofsinger, 1989; Pomerantz, 1989; Schegloff, 1989). The cause of the interview's confrontational character, put simply, was that Bush sought to restrict the interview agenda to his presidential candidacy while Rather, seeing himself as acting in the public interest, sought to question Bush on his involvement in a secret arms-dealing affair which had recently come to light. Known as the Iran-Contra affair, this involved covert deals brokered by the US Secret Service to deliver arms to Iran in exchange for the release of American hostages in Lebanon, and the subsequent use of diverted funds from those deals to support right-wing armed forces in Nicaragua (Lynch and Bogen, 1996). Aware of how this could impact negatively on his candidacy, Bush consistently attempted to steer Rather away from that question.

I will focus on just one extract. We will see that the IR, in accordance with the conventions of neutralism outlined in chapter 4, seeks to preface his question using statements. However, the IE does not observe the corresponding convention of treating statements as prefatory to questions, but instead persistently seeks to "answer" the statements themselves.

"It's a Simple Question"

(1) CBS: Rather-Bush

```
1    IE:   ...I've answered every question put before me.=Now if you
2          have a question, .hh [(what is it.)]
4    IR:                        [ I   do   ha]ve one.
5    IE:   Ple[ase]
6    IR:      [Ah-] I have one. .hh[hh You have said that- if you=
7    IE:                              [Please  fire  away heh-hah
8    IR:   =had know::n, you said tha' if you had known this was
9          an arms for hostag[es sw]ap, .hh that you would've=
10   IE:                     [ Yes ]
11   IR:   =opposed it. .hhhh You also [said thet-
12→  IE:                                [ E x a c t ly
13   IR:   [[that you did NOT KNOW thet y-
14→  IE:   [[(m-    may-    may I-) may I answer that.
15         (0.4)
16   IE:   Th[uh right (    )-
17→  IR:     [That  wasn't a] question.=it w[as a statement eh-
18→  IE:                                    [Yes  it  was  a
19→        statement [and I'll  answer  it. Thuh  President=
20→  IR:             [Let me ask the question if I may first
21   IE:   =created this program, .h has testified er s:tated
22         publicly, (.) he did not think it was arms fer hostages.
23         .hh [and  it  was  only  later thet- and  that's me=
24   IR:       [That's thuh President Mr. Vice President
25   IE:   =(.hh)[Cuz] I went along with it because ya know why Dan?
26   IR:        [We-]
27   IE:   .hh because I:[worried  when  I   saw   Mister: .hh=
28→  IR:                 [That wasn' thuh question Mr. Vice President
29   IE:   =Mister Buckley, (.) uh: heard about Mister Buckley
30         being tor:tured ta death. Later admitted as (a) CIA
```

```
31          chief. .hh So if I erred, I erred on thuh side of tryin'
32          tuh get those hostages outta there.
```

Let us just remind ourselves of one of the principal conventions of interview practice by which neutralistic questioning (that is, questioning which can be probing or challenging while nonetheless maintaining the appearance of impartiality) gets done. As outlined in chapter 4, this relates to the use of statement-formatted question prefaces by interviewers:

1. Interviewers may use statements but only in the framework of putting a question (i.e., as question-prefaces)
2. Interviewees should refrain from speaking until a question has been asked (i.e., treat statements as prefatory to questions)

Note that extract (1) begins with the IE instructing IR, if he "ha[s] a question" to "please fire away" (lines 1–2 and 7). Rather's attempted line of questioning so far has been to establish that Bush, though he denies it, was somehow involved in the covert Iran-Contra arms deals. He begins, in lines 6–11, to form up a question along similar lines using a technique which Pomerantz (1989), in her analysis of other parts of the same broadcast, has described: namely to get the IE to agree to two contradictory factual statements, and then ask a question which invites the IE to deal with the contradiction foregrounded in the statements just agreed to. This kind of *negative pre-positioning* will be seen to be quite commonplace in adversarial and hybrid interviews in this and later chapters. For present purposes, let us note that it is a practice that is consistent with neutralism convention (1) above.

However, in line 14 IE breaches the corresponding convention (2), by interrupting IR's second factual statement ("you also said thet- that you did NOT KNOW . . . " lines 11–13) with an attempt to "answer" the first ("may I answer that"). Notice how, in the following turns, both parties display their hitherto tacit knowledge of the very norms that are being breached, and on which the properties of this occasion as an interview rely: in line 17 IR says "That wasn't a question.=it was a statement" and, in line 20, "Let me ask the question if I may first"; while IE clearly displays that he is moving outside the question-answer turn-taking framework in his intervening utterance: "Yes it was a statement and I'll answer it" (lines 18–19).

It seems clear that in seeking to "answer" a "statement," the IE is displaying some kind of recognition of the IR's adversarial question-building technique, which aims to position him in a way that will inevitably trip him up, or make him appear somehow slippery or evasive. This is a common strategy in many types of political interview (Bull, 2008). In intervening to respond to the first of what is likely to be two conflicting prefatory statements, the IE seeks to derail that strategy, and in the process, exert control over the interview's agenda.

By the end of the extract, Rather has still not managed to put the question he was attempting to ask (line 28: "That wasn' thuh question Mr. Vice President"). Notice, however, that Bush, by holding the floor through Rather's attempts to re-initiate the question, has succeeded in making a powerful political point in the context of his leadership campaign: "So if I erred, I erred on thuh side of tryin' tuh get those hostages outta there" (lines 31-32). In other words, here is a patriotic and humane politician who, if he did make any mistakes, should be forgiven because his overall aim was to get American hostages released, especially in the light of one of them having reportedly been "tor:tured ta death" (line 30).

This extract gives just a glimpse of the way that this interview, in the course of its nine-minute broadcast, came to be widely perceived as a confrontation between the two participants. As with many of the examples discussed in the present chapter, its confrontational tenor led to it being treated to wider media scrutiny, though in a different way from the gaffes considered in chapter 3. In examples like this one, examination in the wider media ecology tends to focus on the nature of the event as "an interview," and the conduct of the individual participants in either maintaining, or disrupting, that event as edifying for the public.

For example, it might be questioned whether the interviewer is being volatile or over-aggressive, even argumentative, and the interviewee merely seeking to provide reasonable responses to whatever it is the interview is supposed to be about. On the other hand, is the interviewer legitimately probing an interviewee who is repeatedly evading answering the question, and therefore conducting responsible public interest journalism in the face of uncooperative behavior from the politician?

In the Bush-Rather example, as Clayman and Whalen (1989: 242–3) describe it, much media commentary at the time surprisingly took Bush's side, Rather being seen as "combative" and "volatile," while Bush "appeared surprisingly forceful and aggressive, and was widely felt to have dispelled his 'wimp' image."

Going beyond these "good guy/bad guy" characterizations, what CA allows us to do is examine in close detail *how* the interview turned into a confrontation; how the situation emerged from a series of departures from the otherwise collaboratively sustained conventions of the interview (Schegloff, 1989). Close analysis shows how, while the consistently overlapping talk could potentially be described as orderly in terms of the much less constrained turn-taking system for ordinary conversation (Sacks et al, 1974;

Jefferson, 1986), it was not orderly in terms of the more formal turn-taking system for news interviews. Quoting Clayman and Whalen again,

> Since contributions to interaction are contingent upon the independent actions of others, they cannot be treated as the straightforward behavioral realization of preplanned political strategies or psychological predispositions. Whatever prior agendas or predispositions there may have been, the actual course of the encounter must be treated as an emergent and fundamentally *interactional* achievement. (Clayman and Whalen, 1989: 243)

PURSUING THE QUESTION

In contrast with our previous example, in which the asking of a question was repeatedly headed off by the interviewee, the next set of examples feature a much more common scenario in adversarial interviews: the asking of a question which is then not answered to the IR's satisfaction, followed by a pursuit of the same question, often over more than one iteration (Romaniuk, 2013).

In the next extract, from an interview with a Serbian nationalist being investigated for his role in the Bosnian war of 1992–1995, we find a series of questions from the interviewer which are not answered straightforwardly by the interviewee, who ends up asking, in line 19, whether the interaction he is involved in is "a cour:t (.) or: a: interview." The IE thus attempts to police the boundaries of the interaction by implying that the IR's line of questioning is tantamount to a cross-examination.

```
(2) Newsnight: Paxman-Bokan

1→    IR:     Mister Bokan, are you prepared to make yourself
2             available to UN investigators?
3             (.)
4     IE:     .hhhh Ah: first of all: I: just want to say that it's
5             you know very strange you know, to hear all those
6             accuses.=And ah:.hhh ah: it's v(h)ery strange to be in
7             the (passive) role:: o:f hearing, an:d ah .hh ah not to
8             have an opportunity you know to:: say anything: uh
9             .hhh ah about yourself or: you know your: ah goals.
10            in war .hh an:d [ah:
11→   IR:                     [I'm not interested in your goals
```

```
12            Mister Bokan.=The question wa:s are you prepared
13            to make yourself avai:lable to UN investigators.
14    IE:     .hhh You know uh- you know: the answer, you know: uh
15            maybe better than ah m:yself. .hhh Because: o::f
16            >you know from the beginning of war,< .hhh I: have
17            just uh one goal an:d that's t'defend you know my people:
18            from the (lynch)=
19→   IR:     =Is that a yes or n:o?
20            (0.5)
21→   IE:     Uh: Is it a cour:t (.) or: a: interview
```

What is it that leads the IE to claim that what he is being subjected to may be closer to a court than an interview? Put simply, what we see in this extract are three of the main features of adversarial interviewing. First, the IR constructs his question in lines 1–2 as a *polar* (yes/no) question ("are you prepared to make yourself available to UN investigators?"). Such a question, of course, sets up a constraint that the IE should respond by saying whether he is, or is not, willing to make himself available. However, second, the IE produces what in CA is called a *non-type-conforming* response: that is, an answer that does not in fact provide the projected yes- or no-type response. Instead, he complains about the accusations leveled against him, and indicates that what he feels he should be asked about are his "goals in war" (lines 4–10). Third, and finally, the IR dismisses the IE's answer as irrelevant (line 11: "I'm not interested in your goals Mr. Bokan") and repeats, in this case verbatim, the polar question he began with ("The question wa:s are you prepared to make yourself avai:lable to UN investigators"). The pattern is then repeated. Following another non-type-conforming response (lines 13–16), the IR once again pursues a polar response, this time quite explicitly: "Is that a yes or n:o?" (line 19).

It is this repetitive pursuit of a plain yes or no answer, coupled with an overt disinterest in the alternative agenda that the IE seeks to address, that evidently leads the IE to question whether the IR is conducting an interview or a courtroom examination (line 21).

The asking of polar questions is a particularly useful strategy in adversarial political interviewing, for a number of reasons. The polarity of the question draws a specific, usually contentious issue out from the background of related, perhaps more nuanced details constituting the news story. Often, as we will see, the interviewee's response is to attempt to address precisely these backgrounded, more nuanced details. By bringing the issue into sharp focus in this way, the polar question proposes that, far from being nuanced, the matter at hand is quite straightforward and can, indeed should, be answered very simply. Clayman and Loeb (2018: 142) describe such questions as "political positioning questions" through which "not only do politicians get accountably linked to specific viewpoints, but they are often situated in relation to an emergent framework of political alliances or to an emergent boundary separating the sociocultural mainstream from extremism or deviance."

Polar questions are therefore a resource by which politicians can fairly simply be made to appear evasive. As Harris (1991: 88) puts it in her study of interviewee evasiveness, once the yes or no question has been posed, "[any] failure of the politician to produce an explicit 'yes' or 'no' (or the equivalent) response will produce a 'noticeable absence.'" The either/or nature of the question, that is, enables the audience easily to notice the lack of a suitable either/or response. Additionally, of course, repeated failures to answer with "yes" or "no" will tend to heighten audience perceptions of evasiveness: especially if the interviewer, as happens in extract (2) above as well as in the following examples, elects to pursue the question.

Perhaps the most notorious case of polar question evasion and pursuit in a televised interview is the 1997 encounter between BBC journalist Jeremy Paxman and Michael Howard, who was then the Conservative government Home Secretary. The interview's notoriety stems from the fact that, during a two-minute-long segment, Paxman repeated the same question ("Did you threaten to overrule him?"), almost word for word, twelve times in succession, while Howard, as will be seen, used numerous linguistic strategies to produce, on each occasion, non-type-conforming answers.

The interview needs to be placed in context to be properly understood. Following numerous riots and escapes from British prisons, including, especially, Parkhurst Prison, Mr. Howard met the director of the prison service, Derek Lewis, to discuss the future of Parkhurst Governor Mr. Marriott. A contradictory account of this meeting emerged in which Lewis, who had decided that Marriott should be moved to a different prison, rather than, as Howard wished, suspended, claims that Howard "exploded" and threatened to overrule his decision as it would be seen to be politically weak. The problem here was that Howard, as Home Secretary, had no operational role in prison governance and therefore was not entitled, within the remit of his political role, either to overrule or threaten to overrule Derek Lewis. Howard strenuously denied that he had made such a threat. Lewis maintained that Howard had, indeed, threatened to overrule his decision. Howard subsequently dismissed Lewis from his post. The matter was considered serious enough for Howard to be called in front of a parliamentary select committee to account for his actions. Later, he was interviewed about it on BBC's flagship *Newsnight*.

Before coming to the most widely referenced aspect of this interview, the polar question repeat/evasion sequence (mentioned by, *inter alia*, Clayman and Heritage, 2002: 256–257; Matheson, 2006: 121–123; Romaniuk, 2013: 150), it is interesting to note that as he introduces the topic, the IR begins with a *different* polar question, to which, in this case, an unequivocal and type-conforming answer is immediately, and emphatically, given:

```
(3) Newsnight: Paxman-Howard

1    IR:    Erm- (.) Mister Howard ev you: (.) ever (.) lied in any
2           public statement,
3→   IE:    Certainly not. .hh u-I: gave a very full account, of
4           the dismissal of Derek Lewis, to the House of Commons
5           select committee, ...
```

What this short extract demonstrates is that it is not always the case that polar questions are resisted or evaded by IEs. In this case, it of course suits the IE's purpose to respond with a type-conforming answer; indeed, one would expect that the IR, in having asked whether the IE has ever "lied in any public statement," fully anticipates an immediate denial.

But although it might therefore appear to be a somewhat "weak" question, offering the IE an easy opportunity to stress his probity in office, the question in fact begins to reveal the IR's strategy, which is to suggest that, Howard and Lewis having said contradictory things, one of them must be lying.

Later in the interview, we find the following exchange which makes this strategy explicit:

```
(4) Newsnight: Paxman-Howard

1    IR:    E:r, can you help us with this then. .mthh Er, you
2           stated in your statement, er- (.) that er the leader
3           of the opposition had said tha-that I, that is you
4           personally told Mr Lewis the governor of Parkhurst
5           should be suspended immediately, .hhh thut when Mr
6           Lewis objected, as it was an operational matter, .h
7           I threatened to instruct him tuh do it. (0.2) .hh
8           Derek Lewis says, Howard had certainly told me that
```

```
9            the governor of Parkhurst should be suspended, and
10→          had threatened to overrule me. Are you saying
11→          Mr Lewis is lying?=
12    IE:    =e-I have (.) given a full account of this, and the
13           position is, what I told the House of Commons=and
14           let me tell you what the po[sition is
15→   IR:                               [So you a:re saying
16→          Mr Lewis [is ly[ing.
17    IE:             [Le- [Let me tell you what the position is.
```

Here, the IR puts another polar question, "Are you saying Mr. Lewis is lying?" (lines 10–11); however, it is prefaced by a long statement in which he reads out two accounts, one from the leader of the opposition and one from Derek Lewis himself, that support Lewis's version of events. The objective here is to negatively pre-position the IE. In order to answer the polar question, Howard must either stick by his own statement, in which case he can be said to be claiming that Lewis is lying, or accept Lewis's statement as true, in which case his own statement is untrue and he has therefore lied about never having lied in public office.

In order to avoid this dilemma, Howard adopts a strategy which he will continue to deploy as the interview progresses, and which Harris (1991) found to be a common response to polar questions that seek to put the IE on the spot, that is to produce an *indirect* answer which addresses, not the question, but the accountability of the IE's actions in relation to the matter in question. Rather than confirming, or denying, that "Mr. Lewis is lying," he attempts to shift the focus onto his own actions in having given "a full account" before the House of Commons select committee. This strategy is not entirely successful, as, in a good example of how formulations can be used adversarially as well as neutralistically, the IR in lines 15–16 formulates the upshot of the IE's response to mean that he must therefore, in fact, be maintaining that Derek Lewis is lying (note the shift from "Are you saying" to "So you a:re saying").

Harris (1991) found that a relatively high proportion (37 percent) of politicians' answers to polar questions in her sample of broadcast interviews were indirect or agenda shifting. A particularly nice example she uses comes from an interview with Bernie Grant, a black council leader from Tottenham in London in the aftermath of violent confrontations between black London youths and the police (Harris, 1991: 87–88). Grant had been quoted in the press as having said that the police "got a bloody good hiding"—a particularly controversial thing to say in the circumstances since one police officer (PC Keith Blakelock) was brutally murdered during what became known as the Broadwater Farm riots (named after the housing development at the center of events). Grant was interviewed on Channel 4's spotlight interview show *A Week in Politics* about what he meant by the statement, and whether he would defend his choice of words.

```
(5) A Week in Politics: Jay-Grant (From Harris, 1991: 87)

1    IR:   Are you saying that it is not your judgement that they
2          got a bloody good [hiding.
3    IE:                     [I'm saying-
4    IR:   Is that not a phrase you would use.
5    IE:   I'm saying that I was putting forward the point of
6          view, the legitimate point of view of the young
7          people on Broadwater Farm.
8    IR:   When you say it's the legitimate point of view, is
9          it also your point of view.
10   IE:   Well whether it is my point of view or not is not
11         material. What is material is that they have a point
12         of view that must be put...
13   IR:   I think there are a lot of people Mr Grant, from the
14         Home Secretary downwards, who do think it is material
15         whether it is your view as the elected leader of your
16         ward - elected councillor and the elected leader of
17         Haringey Council - so I must ask you again. Is it or
18         is it not your view that the police got a bloody good
19         hiding.
20   IE:   It is my view that the young people of Tottenham acted
21         in self defence against a police provocation that
22         had been going on for a number of weeks...
```

The IR's first question (lines 1–2) is a polar question, but notably one which, through being worded negatively, offers the IE an opportunity to withdraw from his controversial statement. In other words, a positive answer to it would constitute a back-down (e.g., "Yes, that view is something I would not in hindsight maintain"). However, politicians very rarely back down in interviews (partly because the inevitable follow-up question would be something like, "Well then, why did you say it?"). Therefore, the IE declines to withdraw the statement, and instead offers a non-type-conforming response in which he both defends his comment and accounts for his actions by claiming it is not his own view, but the "legitimate point of view" of the Broadwater Farm residents that it is his job (he implies) to represent to the media.

In lines 8–9, the IR treats this as an unsatisfactory response, and presses the IE on whether it is also his personal view that the police "got a bloody good hiding." The previous pattern is then repeated, with the IE declining to respond in polar terms to the IR's polar pursuit (lines 10–12). It is then repeated for a third time. The IR repeats his polar question, this time bringing into play the interests of a number of people "from the Home Secretary downwards" in a straightforward answer, and putting the question in explicit terms (lines 17–18: "Is it or is it not your view . . . "). Once more, the IE avoids answering that specific question, instead seeking to redefine the agenda over what his "view" is, in order again to defend the residents' view that the riots were in self-defense against police provocation.

We thus see further evidence of how the very question of what "the question" is can become the subject of intricate linguistic maneuverings. It is not that interviewees, faced with a problematic polar question to which any straight yes or no answer is going to put them in a difficult position, simply refuse to answer or attempt to shift the topic onto another matter altogether. Although the latter does indeed happen (Greatbatch, 1986), the most widely used strategy, as Harris (1991) shows, is to respond either by proposing that the question as stated is not the most pertinent one in the circumstances, and seeking instead to answer that more pertinent, unasked question; or by proffering accounts for the statements or actions that are being treated as problematic in the IR's question, thereby intending to neutralize it.

We can now return to the Paxman-Howard face-off, where we will see, as the interview transcript unfolds, clear evidence of both of these strategies on the IE's part.

```
(6) Newsnight: Paxman-Howard

1    IR:   You can't both be right.

2    IE:   Mister Marriott, was not suspended. (.) I was

3          entitled to express my view:s, I was entitled to

4          be consult[ed,
```

```
5    IR:              [Did you threaten [to overrule (him)
6    IE:                               [I- I was not entitled
7         to instruct Derek Lewis and I did not instruct him.
8         .hh [and the truth of-
9    IR:      [Did you threaten to overrule [him.
10   IE:                                    [The- the truth
11        of the matter i:s that, Mister Marriott was not
12        suspend[ed. I did not-
13   IR:         [Did you threaten to overrule hi[m.
14   IE:                                         [I did not
15        overrule Derek Le[wis
16   IR:                   [Did you threaten to overrule
17        h[im.
18   IE:   [I took advice on what I could or could not d[o::,
19   IR:                                                 [Did
20        you threat[en to overrule him Mr Howard.
21   IE:            [and I acted scrupulously in accordance with
22        that advice.=I did not overrule D[erek Lewis,
23   IR:                                   [Did you threaten to
24        over[rule him.
25   IE:       [Mister Marriott was not suspended.=
26   IR:   =Did you threaten to overrule him.
27           (0.2)
28   IE:   I have accounted, for my decision to dismiss, Derek
29        Lewis, [in great,
30   IR:         [Did you threaten to overrule him.=
31   IE:   =detail, before the House of Commons.=
32   IR:   =I note you're not answering the question whether you
33        threatened, [to overrule him.
34   IE:              [Well the- thee important aspect of
```

```
35        this, which it's very clear to bear in mind,
36   IR:  I'm sorry I'm gonna [be frightfully rude but-
37   IE:                      [is this.
38   IR:  [[I- I'm so(hh)ry, [it's a straight, yes or no question]=
39   IE:  [[Ye:s you can-    [you can, you can put the question]=
40   IR:  =[and I'd (like a) yes or no a:nswer=did you threaten=
41   IE:  =[and I will, and I will give you an answer.
42   IR:  =to overrule him.
43          (0.5)
44   IE:  I discussed this matter with Derek Lewis. (0.2) I gave
45        him the benefit of my opinion. (0.4) I gave him the
46        benefit of my opinion in strong language. (0.2) .hh But
47        I did not instruct him, because I was not, er entitled
48        to instruct him, .hh I was entitled to express my opinion,
49        and that is what I did.
50   IR:  With respect that is not answering the question, whether
51        you threatened to overrule him.
52   IE:  It's dealing with the relevant point. Which is what I
53        was entitled to do, and what I was not entitled to do.
54        .h An' I have dealt with this in detail, before the
55        House of Commons, and before the select committ[ee.
56   IR:                                                  [But
57        with respect you haven't answered the question of
58        whether you threatened to overrule him.
59          (0.2)
60   IE:  Well, you see, the question is what was I entitled to
61        do and what was I not entitled to do. I was not
62        entitled to instruct him, and I did not, do that.
63   IR:  Right. .h Uh- We'll leave, we'll leave that aspect
64        there.
```

As already noted, this extract is most notorious for the IR's insistent repetition of a single (polar) question: "Did you threaten to overrule him?" We see here that the question is first put, in overlap with the IE's ongoing response to a prior question, in line 5. It is put in more or less the same terms a further eleven times: usually, again, in a position of overlap with the IE's attempts to hold the floor and account for his actions regarding the matter of Derek Lewis; with the final attempt occurring in lines 56–58.

There are three basic phases that can be discerned in how this repeated sequence of question and non-type-conforming response unfolds. The first is between lines 1–13. Here, the basic pattern for the exchange as a whole is already visible. The IE seeks to define the question in terms of what he was, and was not, entitled to do in the circumstances, and to emphasize that Marriott was not, in fact, suspended (recall the contextualizing account provided earlier). It turns out that he will maintain this agenda position, in one form or another, for the rest of the interview extract.

Meanwhile, the IR seeks instead to whittle the matter down to one simple question, with a yes/no answer, namely, "Did you threaten to overrule him?" In this first phase, that question is stated three times in the course of the IE's attempt to outline his own competing agenda (line 5, line 9, line 13).

In the second phase (lines 14–26), it appears as if the IE moves to address, and even to give an answer to, the IR's question. However, in doing so he again attempts to shift the agenda pursued by the IR, as he states in lines 14–15, and again in line 22, "I did not overrule Derek Lewis." It is noticeable that he omits the key phrase "threaten to," thereby, in his appearance of giving an answer, implicitly turning the question itself into something very different: not "Did you threaten to overrule him," but "Did you overrule him?" This not very subtle ploy is swiftly detected by the IR, who in response shifts the prosody of his question, in lines 16, 23, and 26, to emphasize precisely the omitted phrase: "Did you threaten to overrule him."

In the third phase, following the short pause in line 27, the interview takes a slightly different turn in which both participants explicitly orient to the fact that the IE is not answering the question (lines 28–64). In line 28, the IE begins on a new iteration of his earlier statement, that he has given a full account of his actions to the parliamentary select committee. This is overlapped by the IR, in line 30, by another repetition of his question, "Did you threaten to overrule him." In the following few turns, the IR moves into what might be called a meta-position in which he states, four times in succession, variants of the observation that "I note you're not answering the question whether you threatened, to overrule him" (lines 32–33; 38–42; 50–51 and 56–58).

In response to this, the IE develops a third strategy to avoid answering the question, which is to state that the question being asked is not the relevant question, and to instruct the IR on what the relevant question, in fact, is. In lines 34–35 he attempts to indicate what he takes to be the "im*p*ortant *a*spect of this," which is not the question being put by the IR. Later, in lines 44–49, he returns to his original standpoint by describing in detail what he did, and what he was and was not entitled to do, in the meeting with Lewis. And in lines 52–55, and 60–62, he dismisses the relevance of the IR's question by stating, once more, what the "r*e*levant p*oi*nt" is: "the question is what was I entitled to do and what was I n*o*t entitled to do. I was not entitled to instr*u*ct him, and I did not, do th*a*t."

In sum, this extract shows how it is possible (though rare, which accounts for the interview's notoriety) for an interviewer to pursue a polar answer to a polar question through a significant number of iterations. However, it also shows how interviewees may develop, in the course of the interview and in response to the repeated questions, a range of strategies which enable them to avoid producing the required answer while simultaneously giving the impression that the responses which they are, in fact, producing are more pertinent to the issue in question.

ACCOUNTABILITY AND QUOTATIVITY

One common feature of the preceding few extracts is that they are all examples of, in Montgomery's (2007) term, "accountability interviews"—the politician is being held to account for something they either shouldn't have said but did, or should be doing but are not, or shouldn't have done but, allegedly, did, and so on. This is a very common feature in adversarial interviews; though as we will see in the next chapter, such pursuit of accountability is not the only interactional mode within identifiably adversarial interviews.

It is also important to note that in such adversarial pursuit sequences, the participants do not noticeably move out of the basic framework of politeness within which both conventional and adversarial interviews tend to be conducted (Heritage and Clayman, 2002: 151). In particular, we might notice the IR's use of overt politeness tokens in the Paxman-Howard interview: "I'm sorry I'm gonna be fri*gh*tfully rude" (line 36); "I- I'm so(hh)ry, it's a straight, yes or no question" (line 40); or "with res*p*ect that is not answering the question" (line 52). This will become an important difference between adversarial and hybrid interviews in later chapters.

Another feature of the interviews so far considered in this chapter is common across adversarial interviews in general: this is the pursuit of *competing agendas* by interviewer and interviewee. The interviewer typically wishes the interviewee to address a particular agenda regarding the news item at hand, either one that has been set by him or herself, or more usually by the news consensus as it has been developing on that day or for the previous few days. The interviewee, aware of the inevitable pitfalls of acceding to this agenda-setting, has arrived at the interview already armed with their own agenda, on which they have usually been briefed by communications managers. Their role therefore is to press this agenda in competition with the interviewer's.

It is in this environment that the kind of pursuit of polar questions, and the repetition of evasive answers, that were analyzed in the previous section, can so easily take root. However, although they stand out precisely because of the way that they can highlight the interviewee's evasiveness, polar questions are of course not the only questioning strategy used by interviewers in the adversarial context.

I will conclude this chapter by looking in more detail at another interviewer strategy that we have already seen some examples of in the above data: the use of *quotativity* by interviewers. Quotativity refers to the construction of questions, or lines of questioning, which directly quote the on-record words of the interviewee, or of some relevant third party, in such a way as to have the interviewee account for those words in the light of more recent events, or perhaps of a contradictory statement made elsewhere.

In order to illustrate this, I examine an extract from a more recent interview in which, somewhat unusually, the interviewee is being asked to account for the highly controversial actions of a third party, in light of on-record position statements that will be quoted back to him.

In 2020, the Sars-Cov-2 (coronavirus, or Covid-19) virus pandemic swept the globe. In an attempt to suppress this highly contagious disease and protect their health services, many national governments unprecedentedly imposed "lockdowns" of varying severity. The UK was one of the countries that, after initial skepticism about the seriousness of the disease, eventually mandated a nationwide, total shutdown of all but essential aspects of the economy, such as food stores, pharmacies, refuse collections and so on. All other businesses and factories were closed, including gyms, leisure facilities, cafes, restaurants and pubs, workers were furloughed, social gatherings were banned, schools were closed, sports, musical and arts events were canceled, and citizens were instructed to remain in their homes at all times, only leaving for essential purposes such as buying food supplies or, for a short period each day, exercise. Police imposed fines on those found to be breaking the lockdown regulations.

As the lockdown extended into weeks and then months, stories began to emerge of high-profile figures apparently failing to observe their own instructions to the public, including health ministers, other members of parliament, and even one of the scientific advisors whose modeling of the disease epidemiology had convinced the government of the need for lockdown to begin with.

In May it was alleged that Prime Minister Boris Johnson's key adviser, Dominic Cummings, had in contravention of the regulations, driven his wife and child over three hundred miles from London to a second home in Cumbria. Later, a further allegation was that he had driven a further thirty miles or so to a local beauty spot known as Barnard Castle, an activity of the kind expressly forbidden at the time to the general public.

Unsurprisingly, the news media pounced on this breach of the government's own policy by one of its central architects, and people started to ask the inevitable question of whether this was a case of "one rule for them, another for the rest of us."

Although Mr. Cummings subsequently gave a long and detailed statement to the media in which he admitted, and attempted to account for his actions, that account only served to heighten the controversy. For example, it appeared that at the time he drove to Cumbria, his wife was showing symptoms of coronavirus; he claimed that a day or so later, he himself fell victim to the virus, both direct contraventions of the public instruction to self-isolate at home and avoid even trips to buy food if symptoms were showing. He argued that he took the trip to Cumbria in order for his parents to be able to care for his child should he and his wife become incapacitated by the disease. His trip to Barnard Castle, he claimed, was to "test his eyesight" after recovering from the virus, before making the long drive back to London.

The statement did not mollify the media, and over the next week or two the story remained in the headlines. It was in this context that the interview occurred from which the next few extracts are taken. In it, BBC journalist Nick Robinson quizzes the government's Health Secretary, Matt Hancock, about the "one rule for them" interpretation of Cummings' actions.

There are, of course, competing agendas at work throughout this interview. The IR's agenda is to get the IE, as Health Secretary and therefore the politician in charge of the public health rationale for the lockdown policy, to admit that Dominic Cummings broke the rules and has therefore undermined public trust in the government, and potentially fatally damaged the lockdown policy. The IE's agenda, as we will see, is to maintain that whatever Cummings did, it was, in his (the IE's) view, somehow within the published guidelines, and it therefore remains everyone else's moral responsibility to stick to the rules in order to suppress the spread of the virus.

To introduce his line of questioning, the IR begins with a *negative prepositioning sequence* in which the IE is asked to agree with statements which the following question is about to contradict. The IR rhetorically seeks to

check that there is "no sma::ll print" in the government's policy, inviting the
IE to confirm that, if a member of the public experiences any symptoms of
coronavirus, they must indeed stay at home for fourteen days:

```
(7) R4: Robinson-Hancock

1    IR:    I wanna be sure that there's no sma::ll print on this.
2→          .hhh People ca:n't leave home. (.) Fourteen days.
3→          They stay at home.
4           (0.6)
5    IE:    We are instructing people, to sta:y, at, home.
6           .h For that four[teen day period.
7→   IR:                    [They can't dri:ve. They can't
8→          go to a beauty spot.
9           (1.2)
10   IE:    U- mm- Well the instructions are absolutely clear,
11          er- and they are that people should, self isolate,
12          at home, for that fourteen days that's right.
13          (0.4)
14   IR:    Well=you see I remember the la:st time you said that
15          things were very clear, in fact you used the word
16          instruction that you've just u:sed, .hh an' then the
17          prime minister's adviser(s) did something completely
18→         different=Dominic Cummings. .hh Now what will you
19→         sa::y, .h if a member of the public now says yih
20→         can keep yer lockdown. .hh If other people don't
21→         abide by it why on earth, should we. The
22          words, .h quoted by a Conservative MP tuh the
23          prime minister yesterday.
24          (0.5)
25   IE:    .h (.) I think thu- the va:st majority of people,
26          wi::ll, understand, that it is in ev'rybody's
```

```
27          interests that those who are at higher ris:k,
28          er follow these er requests from the NHS these
29          instructions.
```

Note that neither of the IR's first two turns here are constructed as questions. Nevertheless, the pauses in lines 4 and 9 are treated by the IE as inviting confirmation of the IR's statements. It is interesting to note the difference in length between the two pauses. The much longer second pause (line 9) comes after the IR has referred to "a beauty spot," thereby making oblique reference to the misdemeanors of Mr. Cummings. The lengthier pause, along with the slight perturbation in the IE's construction of his response ("U- mm- Well") offers an indication that the IE senses, on the interactional horizon, a question that is going to place him in a contradictory, or at least very difficult, position.

That question indeed arrives in lines 18–21. After a further negative prepositioning move in which the IR now explicitly mentions Dominic Cummings having done "something completely different" from the government's "instructions," the IE is asked to respond to the quoted words of a member of the public, essentially voicing the "one rule for them" reaction and proposing that Mr. Cummings' breach of the lockdown rules means that public adherence to the government's instructions may be irrevocably undermined.

The IE's main strategy in response to this line of questioning, which we see in lines 25–29 above, is to state that it is in "ev'rybody's interests" that the public continue to follow the government's instructions. It is, however, notable that, in line 28, he subtly shifts both the way these instructions are described, and their institutional source. Having previously attributed authorship of the instructions directly to the government (line 5: "We are instructing people, to sta:y, at, home"), he now describes them as "requests" which have been issued by a different agency, "the NHS" (National Health Service). Although he subsequently reverts to the stronger term "instructions" (line 29), the shifting of the source away from government and to the NHS could be heard not only as distancing himself and the government from responsibility over the instructions, but as turning the issue into a moral imperative, as the requests or instructions are now said to come from one of the cherished British public institutions, whose workers are daily on the front line of caring for sufferers of the virus.

As the interview proceeds, both IR and IE continue to pursue the agendas established in the previous excerpt. The difference is that the IR's strategy becomes more directly aggressive, as he seeks to use quotativity in a series of repeated questions which is reminiscent of the strategy used in the Paxman-Howard interview, above.

```
(8) R4: Robinson-Hancock

62   IR:   Did Dominic Cummings do the right thing to
63→        use your phrase?
64         (0.8)
65   IE:   .hh Erm I- I think- as I've said befo:re,
66         erm I've answered that question. Um
67         and [what matters
68→  IR:       [W-Did 'e do the right thing.
69         (.)
70   IE:   Er we[ll I-
71→  IR:        [Did 'e do the right thing.
72   IE:   Well [as I said,
73→  IR:        [Did 'e do 'is duty.
```

Here, the IR moves from quoting a member of the public to quoting the IE himself. The question in lines 62–63 quotes a statement attributed to the IE elsewhere in the media, that Dominic Cummings had "done the right thing" in seeking to look after his family when he sensed himself to be under threat of infection with coronavirus. In the light of the preceding exchange, with its focus on the "one rule for them" trope, the question "Did Dominic Cummings do the right thing to use your phrase" clearly seeks to position the IE as supporting the view that whatever Cummings did, it was "right" even though it breached the "instructions" that it is "in everybody's interests to follow."

Moreover, having achieved this apparently duplicitous moral positioning for the IE, the IR does not let up. Instead, each time the IE hearably embarks on a response, he repeats his question: "Did 'e do the right thing" (line 68); "Did 'e do the right thing" (line 71); and then the still more morally judgmental: "Did 'e do 'is duty" (line73).

The IR's series of overlapping pursuits is an example of what Jefferson (2018: 222–227), in a study of what she called "post-response pursuit of a response," described as the "barrage." This is a particularly pointed argumentative strategy in which a speaker repeatedly solicits a response to a question, even where a response may in fact be underway. For example, Jefferson discusses the following extract from a talk radio show:

(9) (Jefferson, 2018: 224)

```
1     Host:   Haven't you bothered to check your facts on any of this,
2     Caller: Yes,
3     Host:   Well then you should know, that a Congressman, or
4             any member of the Congress of the United States, is
5             immune to arrest under certain types of charges,
6             during the time the Congress is sitting.
7     Caller: Mmhm,
8→    Host:   Didn't you know that?
9     Caller: But that's ( [          )
10→   Host:              [Didn't you know that,
11    Caller: I (unders-) I know that.
12→   Host:   If you knew that why did you ask me.
```

Effectively, the host's repeat in line 10 of the question in line 8 proposes that no suitable response has been made by the caller, and a response is therefore due. This is in spite of the fact that, as we can see and the radio host can hear, the caller *has* embarked on a response in line 9. In this particular case, it may be that in the caller's initial words, "But that's" the host already detects a failure of the caller to acknowledge that he is, in fact, aware that congressmen are "immune to arrest under certain types of charges." In other words, the utterance in line 9 embarks on a kind of "Yes, I know that, but" response that deletes the first four words. By pursuing a response post the onset of the caller's response, the host re-situates the caller in the position of having to acknowledge whether or not he knows about the immunity; and the caller having duly acknowledged that he does (line 11), the host is then in the position of being able to dismiss the caller's earlier question, or point, as irrelevant (line 12).

In the case of extract (8), we find a series of three post-response pursuits of response (lines 68, 71 and 73). Not quite as extreme, it might seem, as the Paxman-Howard case where there were eleven repeats of the same question. However, the two cases are slightly different. Whereas in the Paxman-Howard interview, the IE does produce answers of a sort following each repetition of the question, in the Robinson-Hancock interview, in extract (8), the IR's barrage of pursuits only allow the IE to get one or two words into a response on each occasion.

Collectively, what this barrage aims to do is not so much to take issue with the IE's counter-assertion or rebuttal of the IR's question, but actually to *prevent* a counter-assertion or rebuttal being made. It does this by means of the recycling of quotative questions. In summary, as Jefferson (2018: 227) puts it, the barrage is an undeniably argumentative tactic: it "lets its recipient know where he stands—he is 'under attack.'"

CONCLUSION

One of the key themes to emerge from the cases discussed in this chapter is the sheer persistence, within adversarial and accountability interviews, of both interviewers and interviewees in pursuing their competing agendas. What we have also seen is that, despite the oft-cited public complaint that politicians completely avoid answering interviewers' questions, it might be more accurate to say that they construct answers to questions that are based on a competing understanding of what, in fact, "the question" is, or should be. In other words, the common perception of politicians' evasiveness derives from their adeptness at answering questions from a different standpoint, or attempting to assert their own authority over how the interview, or a particular question-answer exchange, should be conducted. In the next chapter, I take up this point again, looking at how one particular aspect of turn-design can play a central part in the struggle over competing agendas and epistemic authority in the political interview.

Chapter Six

"So My Position Is . . ."
Explanatory Answers and Agenda Contests

In one of the earliest and most influential conversation analytic studies of "agenda-shifting" in political interviews, Greatbatch (1986) outlined the two most widely used ways in which political interviewees seek to challenge or to change the agenda they perceive to be behind the interviewer's question. These were the "pre-answer" agenda shift and the "post-answer" agenda shift. As the categories themselves suggest, Greatbatch found that it was not that interviewees failed to answer the question; rather, they tended to offer some answer to the question, but also tag on comments from their own agenda, either prior to answering ("Can I first of all say . . . "; "I'll come to that, but first . . . ") or following the answer ("But if I could also just say . . . "; "But what I really want to say is . . . "). Greatbatch (1986: 453–454) found that, unlike openly evasive or non-type-conforming answers, these agenda-shifting procedures were rarely sanctioned by interviewers, because (a) while the agenda-shift is present, it is done in conjunction with providing an answer; and (b) there being some attempt to produce an answer, the agenda-shift does not involve the interviewee violating the turn-taking system of the interview.

This chapter begins from the same topic of interviewees attempting to answer questions from their own standpoint without violating the interview turn-taking system: that is, by producing what seem like cooperative answers and avoiding interrupting the question. However, the key phenomenon here is only sometimes treated as non-violative by the interviewer. What we will see is that the same answering strategy can be treated (a) as benign; (b) as violative in that it reframes or alters the terms of the initial question; or in some cases, (c) as evidence of outright evasiveness by the interviewee, even though a superficially cooperative answer is provided.

"SO"-PREFACED ANSWERS

I focus on a particular linguistic phenomenon that has seen a noticeable growth in recent years; especially, it seems, in the setting of the news interview and other forms of broadcast political discussion. This is what can be called the so-prefaced answer, in which the word "so," rather than being placed at the start of an interviewer (IR) turn to signal a new question, or introduce a formulation (as discussed in chapter 4: "So, what you're saying is . . . "), instead is used to herald an *answer* to the question by the interviewee (IE).

For example:

```
(1) Peston: Mobile phones
1      IR:   There are some who think smart phones should
2            be ban::ned completely from school:::s what's
3            your position on that.
4→     IE:   .hhh So my position is, erm, schools make these
5            decisions actually the- great majority of
6            schools do restrict or ban er mobile phones
7            an' I absolutely support head teachers in
8            doing that
```

In linguistic terms, the "so" in line 4 is both semantically and syntactically redundant; the IE's answer would take a perfectly adequate shape if it began with the following word, "My . . . " The question is, then, given its apparent redundancy, why has it been placed there?

The so-preface phenomenon has attracted a great deal of attention in the popular media from commentators, journalists and other writers, seeking to provide explanations for why people—not just news interviewees—seem so frequently to be beginning their answers with "so."

One of the most widespread claims is that the practice is used to indicate that the upcoming answer is somehow dumbed down, or needs to be preceded by a "backstory" to be understood, and is thereby involved in proposing some form of intellectual superiority over the questioner. Lewis (1999), for example, claimed that the "so" preface actually emerged in the speech of Californian computer technicians working in the Silicon Valley boom of the 1990s. He observed that these generally young adults would answer almost any question, however benign, with a prefatory "so" followed by a backstory. For example: "'Why did you come to Silicon Valley?' 'So . . . I'm from this small town in Iowa'" (Lewis, 1999: 68).

In the same vein, Sterbenz (2014) observed *Facebook* CEO Mark Zuckerberg, similarly associated with Silicon Valley, "notoriously us[ing] 'so' to start sentences. In a [recent interview] he dropped it four times in just the first answer." Again, part of the reason seems to be the perceived need to provide backstory answers. More broadly, as Nunberg (2015) has suggested, this "backstory *so*" has now become "endemic among members of the explaining classes—the analysts, scientists and policy wonks" who appear as experts on TV news.

An alternative account is offered from a psychological perspective by James (2013), who argued that the tendency to preface answers to questions with the particle "so" is related to the contemporary "presentation of self" (Goffman, 1956), in which what Goffman called "face" is increasingly treated as a pre-prepared and packaged performance. In this view, turn-initial "so" is similar to items such as "look" or "listen" as popularized by ex-British prime minister Tony Blair (Fairclough, 2000). It signals something akin to its producer being about to produce an utterance that is to be heard as authentic or "from the heart"; or in a slightly different sense, to deliver an assertion of undisputable fact. For example, TV football pundits can be heard using "Listen" as a preface when asked to comment on a star player; as in: "The team seem to do better when X is playing, don't they?" "Listen, he's a world-class striker . . ."

Such accounts, while not based on any systematic collection and analysis of naturally occurring data, seem to have a persuasive nucleus of truth about them. Basically, they resonate with two main types of sociological or sociolinguistic categories of action. In sociological terms, the first relates to the performance of expertise, and in particular, the embodiment of epistemic superiority (so-called "dumbing down"); the second relates to the presentation of self, and in particular, the protection and preservation of face. Adopting a similar distinction from sociolinguistics, these can be referred to as "positional" and "personal" stances, where the positional stance casts the IE in a professional relationship (usually of superiority) to the IR, and in the personal stance the IE is more on the defensive, or in face-saving mode.

From a very different angle, an interesting perspective on the *so*-preface appears in Irish poet Seamus Heaney's introduction to his acclaimed translation of the epic Anglo-Saxon tale *Beowulf*. Heaney recounts numerous struggles he faced with finding the most appropriate idiom in which to render the text into contemporary English. This, it turns out, occurred with the very first word of the poem:

Conventional renderings of *hwæt*, the first word of the poem, tend toward the archaic literary, with "lo", "hark", "behold", "attend" and—more colloquially—"listen" being some of the solutions offered previously. But in Hiberno-English Scullion-speak, the particle "so" came naturally to the rescue, because in that idiom "so" operates as an expression that obliterates all previous discourse and narrative, and at the same time functions as an exclamation calling for immediate attention. So, "so" it was:

So. The Spear-Danes in days gone by
And the kings who ruled them had courage and greatness.
We have heard of those princes' heroic campaigns. (Heaney, 1999: xxii)

Not surprisingly, when we look at how "so" is discussed in modern dictionaries, we do not tend to find this kind of usage among its numerous possible functions. "So" tends to be defined either in its adverbial sense ("that view is so beautiful"; "times change and so do people"), or as a conjunction ("it hurt, so I called the doctor"; "it was dark, so I couldn't see him"). But it is Heaney's sense of the term as "heralding" a new beginning or at least the start of some particularly significant line of talk that I want to take forward into the analysis of *so*-prefaced news interview answers, by transposing it into a more conversation-analytic idiom. Thus, we might posit that "so," placed in turn-initial position following a question, can be seen as a particle marking a juncture between what comes before it, which in Heaney's term it "obliterates" (used in the slightly arcane sense of *to wipe out or cover over*), and what comes after, which is to be heard as worthy of a recipient's (or more collectively, an audience's) attention.

Broadly speaking, I show that while *so*-prefaces often herald turns which are identifiably answers to the question, the "so" preface in general seems to mark that the upcoming answer will be somehow non-straightforward, seeking to reframe the question in the IE's terms, either by prefacing what I will call "explanatory answers," or answers that seek to reposition "what is actually important."

TURN-INITIAL PARTICLES

In conversation-analytic terms, the so-preface is an example of a turn-initial particle (or TIP). These are lexical items such as *oh, well, look, listen, so* in English (Bolden, 2006, 2008, 2009; Heritage, 1984; Heritage and Sorjonen, 1994), with variants in numerous other languages such as German (Depperman, 2013), Russian (Bolden, 2018), Japanese (Hayashi, 2009), Polish (Weidner, 2016) or Estonian (Keevalik, 2012). They are placed at the beginning of turns in conversation even though they do not have any necessary syntactic connection with, or semantic contribution to, what transpires in the turn. Despite this, conversation analysts have shown that TIPs have a wide range of distinctive functions in the context of (a) the design of sequences, (b) the management of recipient design between participants, and (c) the ongoing production and reproduction of social relations and relations of knowledge in everyday interaction (Heritage, 2013; Heritage and Sorjonen, 2018).

TIPs can occur either in first position, that is, at the start of turns that initiate a new sequence ("*So*, how was school today?"); or in second position, that is, at the start of turns that provide a response to a prior turn ("*Oh*, nothing special"). Given that the so-prefaced answer is, by definition, a second position utterance, one question might be whether it functions in a similar way to other second position TIPs. A significant body of work has shown that, when used as prefaces to answers, "turn-initial components [are used to] take up stances that resist, or otherwise 'push back' on, some aspect of the prior question" (Heritage, 2013: 333).

However, within this general framework, there are distinct variations in the degree, as well as the kind, of "push back" that different TIPs are involved in. In fact, it might be better to describe these items as marking some form of disjuncture, rather than strictly push-back or resistance, in relation to the prior turn. For example, "Oh" seems to be used when a speaker seeks to mark "repair": for instance, a change of state in their understanding of the prior speaker's action or agenda, or some other shift in their grasp of an informational terrain (Heritage, 1984). "Well" has been shown to be centrally involved in marking dispreferred responses, as well as resisting or rejecting the terms of a prior speaker's perceived action (Pomerantz, 1984; Schegloff and Lerner, 2009). "Look" and "listen" are less widely analyzed at present, but intuitively they seem to mark more overt challenges to a prior speaker, or confident self-assertion on the part of their producer.

In the rest of this chapter, I explore a range of ways in which the particle "so," used as a preface to an answer in news interviews, acts as a disjunct marker that "heralds" some kind of restart, resetting, or reformatting of the prior question, in such a way that the interviewee can be seen to be speaking from a position of epistemic authority, maintaining or establishing their own agenda in opposition to that of the interviewer, or otherwise evading the question.

EXPLANATORY ANSWERS AND EPISTEMIC PRIVILEGE

In one set of extracts, we find the IE using a so-preface to embark on answering in such a way as to treat him or herself as in possession of knowledge, information or expertise which the question, whether implicitly or explicitly, requires them to explicate. In other words, the IE seeks to take up a position of epistemic authority regarding the topic or agenda being pursued by the IR. I will refer to this as *explanatory answering*.

Extract (2) is from a discussion about whether a "People's Assembly" would be a good idea for resolving certain complex political matters. Like a number of examples below, the context for the discussion is the aftermath of the 2016 EU Referendum, where British voters were asked whether they wished to leave or remain members of the European Union (so-called Brexit).

```
(2) TW: People's Assembly

1    IR:    .hhh (0.2) E:r, there would be two 'undred en fifty
2           people?
3    IE:    Yes.=
4    IR:    =H:how would they be chosen.
5           (.)
6→   IE:    So, it's a- process called sortition, .hh it's the
7           same process we use for jury selection=what you
8           would do:, is pick twenty thousand people, from
9           the electoral registe:r,
((lines omitted re details of how 'sortition' works))
10   IE:    It is a genuinely representative random process,
```

In this case, we can notice that the IE has in fact been invited by the IR to provide an explanation: in line 4 he asks her how the participants in the People's Assembly (of which he establishes in lines 1–2 there would only be two hundred and fifty) would be chosen.

What is of interest is the way that the IE provides that explanation. Following a "So" preface, the wording used, "it's a- process called sortition," implies that this is not a process with which the IR, and/or the overhearing audience, is likely to be familiar. Were her recipients to be positioned as knowledgeable about "sortition," a more likely wording would have been something like, "We'll be selecting the participants using sortition." The answer therefore is constructed from the outset as one in which a particular epistemic asymmetry is in play: the IE claims knowledge of what "sortition" is that the IR, via the phrase "it's a process called," is positioned as lacking.

Within this framework, the answer goes on to foreground "explanatory materials" that describe the rules and procedures according to which the process of sortition works.

Extract (3) is slightly more complex. Here, the IR is pressing the IE on the question of whether the government is being inconsistent in abiding by one "instruction" from Parliament (called the Brady Amendment), but not another (to block from negotiations the possibility of a "no-deal" Brexit) (lines 1–7):

```
(3) QT: Brady amendment

1     IR:    It seems that you:, the government, listened
2            to .h one set of instructions, .h e:r which was
3            in the form of an amendment from Graham Brady
4            but you aren't reacting or responding to the
5            other ins[truction, which was to take no deal=
6     IE:              [Hm!
7     IR:    =off the table.=
8     IE:    =No I think the government's been clear all the
9            way through, .hh no deal is not the government's
10           policy, .h we are abs[olutely not, pushing,
11    IR:                         [When will it become the
12           policy when will it become inevitab[le de facto=
13→   IE:                                       [So-
14    IR:    =po[licy.
15→   IE:       [So- (.) What any competent government has to
16           do is to prepare fuh all eventualities. .h The
17           legal default is that we leave without a deal on
18           the twenty ninth of March, .h so we have to
19           prepare fuh that becoz, .h we cannot predict, .h
20           what will happen between now and then that takes
21           it off the table. .h Becuz until it happens,
22           it hasn't happened.
```

In lines 8–10, the IE takes issue with the IR's accusation by stating that there is no inconsistency ("the g̲overnment's been c̲lear all the way through") in that "no de̲al is n̲ot the government's po̲licy." Pursuing the point, the IR puts a question implying that, at some point (i.e., when the deadline for striking a deal runs out), "no deal" will become "inevitable de facto policy."

It is at this point, with a first attempt in line 13 and then a second in line 15, that the IE produces a so-prefaced answer in which she takes up an instructive stance (hence, again, one which implies some form of epistemic authority), explaining what "any competent government has to do." Here, her aim is to reframe the question so that it is not about government policy, but about government competence, specifically the need to prepare for leaving without a deal in the face of the "l̲egal default . . . that we leave without a deal on the twenty-ninth of March."

In other examples, we find so-prefaces heralding answers that seek more explicitly to reframe the question and answer it on their own terms. Consider extract (4):

```
(4) PL: Indicative Votes

1      IR:    How wi̲ll these indi̲cative votes as they're called

2             wo̲rk. in o̲r:der to try an' fi̲:nd, .h an o̲ption,

3             .h that Parliament li̲kes by a majority.

4→            (0.2)

5→     IE:    .mthh So::- thee- di̲fficulty that indi̲cative

6             votes a:re, sortuv inte̲nded to try and get aro̲und
```

Here the IE embarks on an answer in a way that subtly differs from the way the preceding question has been put. Having been asked how indicative votes will "work" (lines 1–2), the IE begins instead by describing what the votes are intended to *do*: namely, to "get aro̲und" some difficulty (lines 5–6).

Notice that the IE's turn is preceded by a slight pause. Even pauses of less than half a second have been shown to act as markers indicating an upcoming dispreferred answer (Davidson, 1984; Pomerantz, 1984). In this instance such a dispreference marker may indicate that the IE sees the question as one that can best be answered by first asserting their own knowledge of its topical field. However, the turn is not hearably "evasive" since it projects that the answer will be provided, albeit in a different format to that projected by the question.

This becomes slightly clearer if we look at how the answer in extract (4) proceeds:

```
(4)  (Extended)

1    IR:    How will these indicative votes as they're called
2           work. in or:der to try an' fi:nd, .h an option,
3           .h that Parliament likes by a majority.
4           (0.2)
5    IE:    .mthh So::- thee- difficulty that indicative
6           votes a:re, sortuv intended to try and get around
7           is the fact that a:ll votes in Parliament are
8           binary.=they're yes an' no:. .hh An' that is a
9           very blunt instrument to try and get at what
10          people's sortuv second or third choices might be
11          an- and to try to identify compromises. .hh We
12          don't know exactly what the process is going
13          to be yet,((continues))
```

As we see, the IE uses her initial reformatting of the question as the starting point for an answer which, instead of addressing the IR's question of how the votes will work, addresses the IE's preferred agenda which is to describe the problem of binary votes which are a "blunt instrument." Only once that work is done does she return, in a tangential way, to the IR's agenda, indicating that in fact it is not yet known "exactly what the process is going to be" (lines 12–13).

These extracts show the IE orienting to the need to provide technical or other forms of background knowledge to which they have unique access, before the question can in fact be answered. This often involves reformatting the way the question has been put, whether in terms of its terminology, its technical complexity, or its technical backstory.

AGENDA RESETS, MY-SIDE TELLINGS, AND EVASIONS

In a further collection of examples, so-prefaced answers are used in ways that attempt to evade the question, or alter the agenda being pursued by the IR, often by contrasting some claim, assumption, or aspect of the question's wording with what the IE him or herself thinks (a "my-side" telling).

A particularly clear example is the following, taken from the run-up to the 2020 US presidential election. During the campaign, Donald Trump had tested positive for coronavirus, but after only a short stay in the hospital, he was filmed in an official car driving past his supporters who had gathered outside, wearing a mask and waving from behind the closed windows. The IE, a representative of the activist group Black Voters for Trump, is asked about the medical ethics of this:

```
(5) NewsNight: Trump Drive-by

1      IR:    Can I just a:sk you about that image yesterday
2             because it has left quite an inden:t, .h an'
3             it was called irresponsible by the medical
4             staff at the hospital in which he was being
5             treated. .hh He was an infected ma:n, in a
6             hermetically sealed car, (.) with, members of
7             his sta:ff, (.) w- why would he: why would
8             he do that tuh people, (.) that work fer him.
9→            (2.3)
10→    IE:    So:: hhh. My name's Stacey Washington? I'm
11→           not actually Donald Trump. But I am here to
12            give the positive message, that the president
13            is seeking the vote, of Americans, he's not
14            demanding it, he's never said that black
15            Americans .h owe him their vote if we don't,
16            I'm not black if I don't vote fer Joe Biden=
17            that's what 'e said about me=Joe Biden said
18            I'm not from a diverse community, Hispanics
19            have a diverse community blacks do not,...
              ((continues))
```

The IR's question heavily implies a critique of President Trump's actions. For example, medical staff "at the hospital" called the actions "irresponsible," and there is a suggestion that, as an "infected ma:n," by being in a "hermetically sealed car" Trump was putting his security staff at immediate risk of contracting the virus. In this sense, it is hearably loaded against the IE, an avowed Trump supporter. The use of loaded questions is commonplace in adversarial and accountability interviews: we saw numerous examples in the previous chapter and more will be found in the next. One of the interesting things about them is how interviewees elect to respond to them.

Here, in lines 9–11 the IE begins by leaving a noticeable silence (2.3 seconds) between the IR's question and her embarkation on a response. That response is then prefaced with an extended "S<u>o</u>::" and an audible outbreath ("hhh"). These three features combine to convey an impression of annoyance at the question. More to the point, however, what the "so" prefaces, in this case, is the IE embarking on an explicit agenda reset using a my-side telling, literally describing who she is ("Stacey W<u>a</u>shington?") and, by contrast, who she is not ("Donald Tr<u>u</u>mp"). By these means, she indicates that she is not going to accept the invitation to speculate on the motives behind Trump's decision to make the drive-by. Evading the question entirely, then, the IE embarks on a lengthy account of what she *is* going to talk about, namely a positive message about Trump and black voters.

In extract (6), there is in fact clear evidence that in some circumstances, the very production of a so-prefaced answer can be treated by the IR as a marker of upcoming evasion even before anything substantive has been said (see also extracts 7 and 9 below):

```
(6)  QT: EU backstop

1     IR:     What this is hinging on is-is: Theresa May
2             going back to (.) the EU to try: an' see if
3             she can sort something new about the
4             backstop. .hh La::st, (0.2) summer, she said,
5             no technology solution to address these
6             issues has been desi:gned yet, .h or
7             implemented anywhere in the world,=.h=let
8             alo:ne, .hh in such a unique and highly
9             sensitive context as the Northern Ireland
10→           border. (0.3) What's cha:nged.
11→   IE:     .hhh So, I mean=.h I don't think sh[e means-
12→   IR:                                        [Seriously
13→           what- what 'as cha[nged.
14    IE:                       [So she- she's not
15            suggesting it's going to be easy but there
```

```
16              are clearly [places,
17    IR:                  [Wull she is she's saying it's
18              impossible.
19    IE:       Well, there er c-=there er clearly a set of
20              options to explore,
```

The IR's question in line 10 is preceded by a detailed account which places prime minister Theresa May in a contradictory position, which she is about to ask the IE to account for. According to the IR, May is claiming to be able to "sort something new about the backstop" (a complicated technical solution for the avoidance of a border between Northern Ireland, part of the UK, and the rest of Ireland, which remains part of the EU); however, she earlier insisted that "no technology solution" to this question currently exists "anywhere in the world." As we have already seen, this kind of negative pre-positioning is a standard adversarial practice among IRs (Pomerantz, 1989). In the context of these contradictory statements, after a short pause, she puts the question: "What's cha:nged."

As we see, hearing the IE embark upon a response with a so-preface (line 11), the IR swiftly breaks in to restate her question (line 12), thereby treating the very first, uncompleted part of the answer ("So, I mean=.h I don't think sh[e") as identifiably an attempt to avoid addressing "what's changed." Nonetheless, the IE restarts her answer, again using a so-preface (lines 14–16) and moves on, in the face of a further combative interjection from the IR, to the substance of her response (there are "a set of options to explore").

Extract (7) shows an IE more clearly seeking to resist or at least push back on the IR's agenda, using a so-prefaced response. Again, the IR intercedes prior to the completion of the first part of the IE's response, seeming to treat the so-prefaced response as evidence of possible evasion:

```
(7) QT: Sex education
1     IR:    When it- comes to teaching (0.2) five year
2            olds six year olds, .hh about same sex relations
3            >um not talking sex education< but about same
4            sex relationships.=An' this is where, .h some
5            schools uv had problems with parents who've
6            objected. .hh Do you support that.
7            (1.8)
```

```
 8→   IE:   So, can I- ↑can I just take one ste[p back,
 9→   IR:                                        [ Well.
10→   IR:   =Do you [or don't you.]
11    IE:           [ an'  sa:y,  ] No, cuz it's not that
12           simpl::e eh you can't make all these questions
13           into binary, questions they are complex questions
```

Having been asked a polar (yes/no) question as to his support for the policy of teaching young schoolchildren about same-sex relations, and following a pause, the so-preface leads into an attempt to "step back" from that question. The IR treats this as an evasion, or at least as necessitating a restatement of her question, again in polar terms (line 10). From line 11 onwards, the IE persists in his resistance, claiming the issue is more complex than the polar question allows.

Slightly later in the same exchange, once the IE has, in a long turn, set out his position that it is better for young children to learn about such things in school rather than via the internet (lines 1–8 below), the IR returns to the polarity of the question. Here, the IR uses a formulation, beginning in line 9, which, although it is spoken over by the IE attempting to continue with his previous point, presents a claim that the upshot of his position must therefore be that the IE does support the policy (lines 13–14):

```
(8) QT: Sex education

 1    IE:   An' it is much safer, .h to have a child to have
 2           the opportunity to hear about that an' discuss that,
 3           in:, a safe environment, et school, from a teacher,
 4           than it is to pick it up on the internet, or
 5           just to hear what other kids er saying. .hh So
 6           we've just updated relationships an' sex
 7           education guidance, (.) by the way for the first
 8           time in nineteen yea:rs,
 9→   IR:   But so- so th[e- so- surely thee thee thee take]=
10    IE:                 [.h an the way the world's changed]=
11→   IR:   =[out from that] is thut- [that it is- it] is o-
12    IE:   =[in that time,]          [is, incredible]
```

```
13→   IR:   i- it is, something that you would support for
14→         children in primary school.
15→   IE:   So the- there isn't a req- So. The way the- the
16          way the guidance is set out there's not a requirement
17          to teach, about (.) particular matters including
18          their LGBT relationships, at a particular a:ge
19          becus we trust teachers, .h to make those, to make
20          those judgements.
```

The IE's response to this formulation, in line 15, is prefaced with a "So." But more than that, having embarked on his turn with what looks like the words "there isn't a requirement," he breaks off one syllable into "requirement" in order to produce *another* "So." It is not immediately clear why the IE does this, although it could be associated with the preceding few turns at talk, which have taken place in overlap and thus, to the audience's ears, may have sounded confusing. By breaking off his response and effectively restarting it with a "So," the IE can ensure that his response is produced fully in clear turn-space. He then uses this turn to continue his resistance to the IR's polar question agenda, emphasizing that the document under discussion amounts to "guidance" and not a "requirement" to teach about same-sex relations, and that "we" (the "corporate we" indicating the government) trust teachers to make the call.

A further clear example of this agenda-resetting combined with a contrastive my-side telling can be seen in the following extract.

```
(9) PL: Labour Reforms

1     IR:   You run an organisation called Reform, (0.2) there
2           was loads of refor:ms here, which ones did you
3           like which ones did you hate.
4           (.)
5→    IE:   So:, I thought that some of the diagnosis, of the
6           problems we're faci:ng was very good. Erm, .hh and,
7→    IR:   Oh, s[o you didn't like any of the reforms. Hm! h .h!
8     IE:        [I::, (.) #I::, e::r, I'll come on to that.
9     IR:   Oka:y,=
10→   IE:   =E::r, so, I think yihknow, I was very struck when John
```

```
11         McDonnell in his speech, talked about giving workers
12         a say an' a sta:ke, an' I think that's absolutely
13         essential=an'if you l:ook at the long tail, .h of
14         the financial crash, .h if you look at, the kind of,
15         .h erm, I know that now wages er now goin- going up,
16         but they actually are a lot lower than they should
17         be, if you look at families struggli:ng, .h erm if
18         you look at the .h shift of power (0.2) on the whole
19         towards big business and not, (0.4) workers, .hhh
20         I think that's (.) an important thing to talk about.
21→        .hh Do I think some of the solutions that've been
22→        put forward are right, no I don't.
```

The IE is invited to assess the reforms put forward at the recent Labour Party conference, again through a form of polar question (like vs. hate). However, her so-prefaced response subtly shifts this agenda to address the "diagnosis" of the country's problems, through a my-side telling. As in the above extracts, the IR comes in without waiting for the second part of the projected contrast (diagnosis vs. reforms), again using a formulation to propose that the IE, by virtue of shifting the agenda toward "diagnosis," indicates that she "didn't like any of the reforms." Though this is followed by a slight laugh ("Hm! h .h!"), with the IE stating in overlap that she will move on to the reforms presently, in fact in lines 21–22 she confirms, through a rhetorical self-directed question, that the IR's inference had been correct.

The next extract shows a striking example of an IR pursuing a line of questioning through what he clearly takes to be a series of uncooperative or evasive responses from the IE. This extract, like the previous two, combines some of the features of adversarial questioning explored in chapter 5, namely the repetition of polar questions and the pursuit of yes/no answers, culminating in a yes/no question which receives a so-prefaced response that simultaneously dispenses with any attempt to answer the question as put, and resets the IE's contribution, once more, into explanatory mode.

```
(10) AMS: Indicative votes

1    IR:   Here's the real question. (.) If indicative
2          votes so called, go ahead next week whether under
3          the control of the government, or under control
```

```
 4           of MPs directly, (.) if those votes go ahead, with
 5           a ran:ge of possible options .h for the future of
 6→          Britain, .h is the government bound by those,
 7→          or not.
 8    IE:    .mth=Well the key question you say is if because
 9           we need t's[ee (how does that go)
10    IR:         [Yah, I'm (looking for) the a:nswer to
11           that que[stion.
12    IE:            [Well firstly we need to see, if- it does
13           go ahead becuz I think the implications .h of that
14           are so severe constitutionally, .h that the- it
15           will be [a serious question for members of=
16    IR:           [Ye-
17    IE:    =Parliament [whether they want to go-]
18    IR:                [It will be but, this is ] a really
19           really important moment fuh the country and
20→          you really need to start to answer questions if
21           I may say so about this kind of thing,=.h=if, the
22           Commons takes control or if there are indicative
23           votes under the control of the cabinet, .h and
24           the Commons votes for a different outcome, .h
25→          is the government bound by that, or not.
26→   IE:    .mth=So:: the process will be: that we will have
27           an all day debate on: Monday, ahead of that vote,
28           now if that vote goes through, .hh and the House
29           of Commons does take control, of the order paper,
30           .h then under the process there will then be
31           indicative votes, .h er on Wednesday,
```

The IR first puts his polar question to the IE in lines 6–7: "is the government bound by [the results of indicative votes] or not." The IE begins on a hearably evasive response (lines 8–9) which prompts the IR to reiterate that what he seeks is "the a:nswer" to the question (lines 10–11). Following further evasive talk in which the IE seeks to focus on the constitutional implications of the so-called indicative votes, the IR returns the agenda emphatically to his question (lines 18–21). Having stated in strong terms that the IE "really need[s] to start to answer questions," (line 20) he puts the question, once more, in a polar form, "is the government bound by that, or not" (line 25).

Even in the face of this sustained attempt by the IR to indicate (a) that the IE is avoiding the question, and (b) that the issue is so important for the country that there is almost some kind of moral duty upon him to answer it, the IE continues his avoidance of the IR's agenda. In line 26, notably, he does this by producing a so-prefaced response in which, rather than answering the question in positive or negative terms, he embarks upon a *description* of the technical process of "indicative votes" that the House of Commons is about to embark upon. In this move, we find the IE once again utilizing exactly the kind of "explanatory" so-prefaced answering that was seen in the earlier extracts.

CONCLUSION

In the previous chapter, I described political interviews as interactional combat zones: arenas of language use in which, within the potentially sterile environment of questions and answers, journalists and political actors engage in thinly veiled contestation over the representation of current political ideas, policies, strategies and agendas. The participants engage in a verbal "competition, and with varying levels of skill . . . deploy their moves strategically in pursuit of divergent goals and objectives" (Clayman and Heritage, 2002: 25).

This chapter has focused on a sequential resource in this discursive competition that seems to have come increasingly into play in recent times: the so-prefaced answer. Accounts of this phenomenon in the popular media have tended to suppose that the practice is used to indicate that the upcoming answer is somehow dumbed down, or needing to be preceded by a backstory to be understood, and is thereby involved in proposing some form of intellectual superiority over the questioner.

There is a nucleus of truth in this. The various uses of *so*-prefacing identified above overlap in the sense that they position the IE not just as respondent to IR questions, but as in possession of unique knowledge, information or expertise which the question, whether implicitly or explicitly, requires them to explicate or expound. What is of interest, however, are the ways in which they *use* that positioning, in singular instances of interaction within the interview, in order to establish their epistemic authority and/or pursue their competing agendas.

The analysis has shown that the so-preface in the news interview context operates along similar lines to other second-position turn-initial particles, in managing a potentially disjunctive relationship between the form and format of the question and its response (Heritage, 2013). We have seen a range of describable types of work the particle does in relation to both the question-answer sequence it is part of, and the social relations between interviewer and interviewee in this setting. Broadly speaking, the so-preface is bound up with the production of answers that seek to depart from the way the question is worded; that are constructed as contrastive as between personal avowals and policy positions; or that are in some way resistant to, or evasive in respect of, the IR's question or broader agenda. Interviewees use so-prefaced answers to frame positional stances that lay claim to superior knowledge in either developing the IR's question (usually through the production of "explanatory answers") or seeking to refute or avoid it.

In the next two chapters we move on to examine a far more aggressive tendency in news interview discourse: the hybrid political interview. Although this form of interview, which increasingly dispenses with the forms of neutralism outlined in the previous chapters, emerged in the context of US cable news in the late 1990s/early 2000s, I will eventually seek to show that aspects of it are beginning to become influential in more mainstream broadcast contexts, as increasingly confident interviewers encounter increasingly bullish, challenging political interviewees.

Chapter Seven

Opinion, Emotion, and Personalization in the Hybrid Political Interview

This chapter addresses a type of televised political interview in which the norms of neutralism are increasingly and overtly dispensed with. In fact, the role of the IR in the data presented below can be characterized in precisely the opposite terms: as expressly "non-neutralistic." In more structural terms, the interviews can be described as a hybrid discourse genre which merges formal news talk with the "confrontation talk" (Hutchby, 1996) of talk radio. I call such a format the *hybrid political interview* (HPI).

The HPI adopts the basic question-answer structure of news interviews, with a studio host addressing questions to a politician or other public figure or spokesperson who is expected to answer them. Yet within that formal structure the interlocutors—most notably and consistently the host—freely move between the speech exchange system of the interview and other speech exchange systems that are more readily associated with disputes or arguments in both conversation and institutional talk. The primary norms of neutralism previously described for conventional *and* adversarial political interviews are repeatedly breached.

Before getting into the detail of this chapter it is important to point out that, although most of the data discussed below are taken from US cable news channels, the phenomenon of hybridization in the political interview is not restricted to that context. For a number of years now, studies have observed the shift toward non-neutrality, and the hybrid forms of argumentative or tendentious interview, in various contexts of political interviewing around the world. For example, research by Ekström and Tolson (2017), Kantara (2017, 2018), Lauerbach (2004, 2010), Patrona (2011) and the studies collected in Mast, Coesemans and Temmerman (2017) all explore different aspects of hybrid political interviews. However, it is probably true to say that the phenomenon is at its most well-developed, and its most extreme, forms in the kinds of data to be discussed below.

To a certain degree the HPI is related to wider trends in the discourse of televised political journalism. As we saw previously, Montgomery (2007) argues that tensions between institutional neutralism (based in the mainstream broadcasters' commitment to a public service remit) and investigative probing (based in the evolution of the journalist's role) are leading some mainstream interviewers to adopt increasingly skeptical stances when addressing certain issues, especially where high-profile politicians are being brought to account for alleged misconduct, public deception and the like; or when marginalized views or extremist political stances are at issue. Here, the questions put by the interviewer may become more assertoric, leading to a perception of reduced neutrality.

The HPI shares some features with accountability interviews but differs in many other respects. Although it displays many of the features of the interview as an institutional discourse form (primarily, the exchange of questions and answers), its very character as a "hybrid" discourse involves systematic shifting between speech exchange systems otherwise associated with non-interview settings. Primary factors involved here include the HPI interviewer's greater license to personalize argumentative standpoints; to foreground his or her agency as a spokesperson "for" certain political stances or social forces; and to engage in belligerent and emotionally heightened episodes of direct confrontation with the interviewee. These are features more readily associated with the activity of arguing.

ARGUMENT AND ADVERSARIALISM

Arguing is distinct from adversarialism in important ways. Adversarialism can involve challenging an interlocutor's line, seeking accountability for statements or positions, pressing for answers and such like; however, it typically does not involve the interviewer, as institutional representative, explicitly taking up a line of their own and pursuing it in opposition to the interviewee's. Adversarial interviewers may use assertoric questions; however, they do not engage in producing the extended chains of assertion and counter-assertion that are characteristic of *arguments* found in conversation (Coulter, 1990) and other settings (Hutchby, 2001b). Lastly, whereas one can be adversarial while remaining neutralistic (Heritage and Clayman, 2002), involvement in chains of assertion and counter-assertion implies the abandonment of such neutralism.

Previous research has shown that there are significant differences between the ways in which disputes are produced in ordinary conversation and in institutional settings such as interviews, debates or mediation hearings (Garcia, 1991; Greatbatch, 1992; Hutchby, 1996). Central to all types of disputatious interaction is the *action-opposition sequence*, in which one speaker's utterance is treated as an *arguable action* that the interlocutor opposes; with the *opposition* move itself then being treated as the arguable action of a next sequence, and so on (Maynard, 1985; Hutchby, 1996, 2001b). In different types of setting, there are differences in the precise ways in which opposition moves are related to their prior actions.

In ordinary conversation, arguments may freely take mitigated or aggravated forms; direct address is frequently used; and oppositional turns are placed contiguously as action-opposition sequences unfold. By contrast, disputes in institutional interaction tend to be overdetermined by specialized speech-exchange systems such as that involving third-party management of turn-taking by a chair or mediator. The result is that oppositional turns tend to be more mitigated than in non-institutional talk; speakers tend to use direct address less frequently; and action-opposition sequences tend to be non-contiguous as the mediator's turns intervene to allocate speaking rights (Garcia, 1991).

The HPI is a distinct "third type" in this array. It is a form of institutional interaction: technically an interview conducted in a television studio. Yet the HPI frequently involves disputes that have the aggravated, directly addressed and sequentially contiguous format of non-institutional argument. My aim in this chapter is to analyze the features of turn-taking and turn-design that contribute to this hybridization of interview and argument.

"THIS IS UNBELIEVABLE": TAKING ISSUE IN THE HYBRID POLITICAL INTERVIEW

The HPI has some affinities with the accountability interview (Montgomery, 2007). Among the similarities between the two types are the following:

1. *Leading questions*: Opening questions are often "leading" —or formulated as first moves in assertion/counter-assertion sequences.
2. *Repetition*: Interviews can revolve around a single question or implied accusation which is put repeatedly and evaded by the interviewee; or is not answered to the interviewer's satisfaction.
3. *Demeanor differentiation*: Interviewees often observably orient to the aggressive demeanor or adversarial behavior of the interviewer. They

may seek to topicalize it by distinguishing their "reasonable" attempts to conduct an interview with the interviewer's "unreasonableness."

4. *Non-resolution*: Interviews often end on an unresolved note. Interviewers can make it clear that the question upon which the interview has been based has not been answered, or has been answered but manifestly not to their satisfaction or, by implication, that of the audience.

However, my aim is to focus principally on the dimensions along which the HPI *differs* from the accountability interview. To do that, it is useful to begin with one example in which we can get a sense of an HPI interviewer "taking issue" with something an interviewee says in this kind of context.

The IE in the following extract is a feminist and editor of the online magazine *salon.com*. She is being interviewed by female journalist Laura Ingraham on the topic of whether feminists should intervene in a debate sparked by responses to a beauty pageant queen (Carrie Prejean), who had been stripped of her title after public statements in which she expressed opposition to the legalization of same-sex marriage.

Once she has introduced the upcoming interviewee, the IR opens the interview in the following manner:

```
(1) O'REILLY FACTOR: Miss California

1    IR:    .mhhh This woman:, Carrie Preje:an, was savaged,
2           last night, on MSNBC:. .hh by Michael Musto, who's a
3           gay writer, apparently for uh the Village Voice,
4           an:d, .h u:h the MSNBC host, .h savaged in the most
5           personal vicious wa:y, .h about her physi::que an-
6           .hh an- and her th-her sexual or(h)gans=uh th-
7           references were ma:de tuh that, .hh an' I'm thinkin'
8           to myself where er the feminists? (.) Are feminists
9           not gunna step up an' say .h=Waidasecond. Yih d-
10          you don't go ther:e,wuh-witha d- with a young woman
11          this is W:::AY oudabounds of even minimal: standards
12          uv decency.
13          (1.5)
14   IE:    .hh We:ll lemme say Laura that, first of a:ll...
```

Opinion, Emotion, and Personalization in the Hybrid Political Interview 119

In lines 1–12, the IR's turn superficially takes the conventional news interview form of a set of statements prefacing a question. However, both the statements and what stands as a "question" in this extract are very different from, indeed in some ways the inverse of, the kind of neutralistic questioning outlined in earlier chapters.

First, the IR's initial statements (lines 1–7) do more than simply present a version of events for the IE to respond to. Instead they act as a preamble which at least implicitly *positions* the IR herself in relation to the issue to be discussed. She refers to Ms Prejean being "savaged" in "personal vicious" ways by the "gay writer" Michael Musto who along with the MSNBC host had responded to this story by mocking the "physi::que and…sexual or(h) gans" of Ms Prejean.

Second, the IR's subsequent action is to pose a question; however, it is a rhetorical question in which she asks *herself* why feminists were not defending Ms Prejean against such attacks, which she evaluates as "W:::AY oudabounds." The pause in line 13, preceding the IE's first turn, is indicative of a possible problem the IE therefore has in identifying the point at which the opening "question" has in fact been posed.

Third, not only is the IR's opening turn full of evaluative phrases, it is also loaded in that it positions the IE, an avowed liberal feminist, in a potentially contradictory position. As a liberal, she could be expected to disagree with Ms Prejean's opposition to same-sex marriage, and thus align with her critics on MSNBC; yet as a feminist, she could be expected to defend Ms Prejean as a woman against sexist comments, and thus align with her against those same critics.

Extract (2) shows the IE's attempt to construct an answer, and more significantly for the present purposes, the IR's response to that attempt:

```
(2) O'REILLY FACTOR: Miss California

1     IE:    ...let me just sa:y, that, uh feminism is about

2            justice and equality..h I think that, that what

3            Miss Prejean needs is perhaps ay heart transplant,

4            rather than the breast impla:nts that she had paid

5            for by the: .hh by the pageant..h To b[e perfectly-

6→    IR:                                          [Waitwohwohwoh

7            So [you're attacking her looks.]

8     IE:       [No::, I-  I-  I  was-    ] No thu this is-

9            this is true en actuall[y,
```

```
10→IR:                           [WHY did you just
11         sa[y that?
12    IE:  [I'm gla:d- No I think that- (.) now she [is fair game.
13→   IR:                                                   [This is
14         unbelievable.
15    IE:  She is now fair ga[:me because she is a national=
16→   IR:                    [eHHHHAAA!=I LOVE it! ((clap-clap))
17    IE   =spokesperson for a group that opposes marriage
18         equali[ty.=.h An' you have to kno::w,
19→   IR:         [This is great! Ay feminist is attacking a woman
20         for how she looks.=Th[is is great. [You guys have come=
21    IE:                       [Yi-          [Yihn-
22    IR:  =full circle here in the United States of America. .hh
23         Now it's okay fer feminists, .h tuh ridicule women,
24         .h fer the wa[y they look.
25    IE:               [I didn't ridicule [her, nor- I didn't=
26→   IR:                                  [Go for it Gloria.
27    IE:  =ridicule her nor do=I know of another feminist who has.
```

The IE's answer in lines 1–5 attempts, utilizing the contrastive device "heart transplant"/"breast implants" to suggest that Ms Prejean should show greater compassion or recognition of difference. However, the reference to her "breast implants" in fact plays into the tendentious way the question had originally been set up by the IR, by appearing to collude with other media commentators who had been critical of Ms Prejean on physical terms.

It is at this point that the IR comes in (line 6) with an utterance that overtly attempts to curtail the IE's turn: "Waitwohwohwoh." This turn is produced interruptively in sequential terms, in that while there is a legitimate transition-relevance place after the IE's words "by the pageant," IE has sought to retain the floor with a continuation of her turn in line 5. Yet the turn is also constructed so as to "do" the work of "being interruptive" in its syntax. Use of the word "wait" indicates that the IR is expecting, or has heard, the IE's continuation with her turn, while the repeated expression "wohwohwoh" seeks explicitly to arrest that continuation.

Following this intervention, the IR produces a standard type of interviewer turn, namely a formulation: "So you're attacking her looks." As we saw in earlier chapters, formulations may be neutralistic, in the sense that they avoid commenting on or making assessments of the content of a prior turn, or inferentially elaborative, looking to make something more of a topic than was originally suggested. In extract (2), the IR uses aspects of the IE's turn (the reference to breast implants) to situate the IE in alignment with what have earlier been presented as the sexist comments of those opposed to her stance on gay marriage.

In news interviews, formulations are also turns that IEs seek to agree or disagree with in their next turn. In line 8, the IE attempts to disagree with the IR's formulation. Before the response can be elaborated, however, the IR comes in with what turns out to be the first in a series of interjections (arrowed) which follow on from the formulation, all of which are produced in overlap with the IE's attempts to assert that Ms Prejean is "fair ga:me because she is a national spokesperson for a group that opposes marriage equality."

A key point about the IR's succession of utterances in lines 10, 13, 16, 19 and 26 is that they are not attempts to put forward further questions to the IE about her position. Rather, they are expressions of a personal standpoint *in relation to* the view that has been formulated, by the IR herself, in line 7 ("So you're attacking her looks.") In this sense, it may be more accurate to say that the IR merely engages in "argumentative talk," rather than the rational exchange of assertion and counter-assertion that is sometimes posited as the basic structure of argument (Coulter, 1990).

In more general terms, extract (2) illustrates a number of ways in which the HPI differs from the more mainstream, though still aggressive, adversarial/ accountability interview (API). These can be summarized as follows:

1. *Personal stance-taking and evaluation*: In the API, IRs may adopt personal standpoints, but still frequently use the adversarial technique of ending the turn with an interrogative ("This is unacceptable, isn't it?" "Isn't that the case?"). In the HPI, IRs may swiftly move from (loaded) opening questions to explicit personal stance-taking with no tag-positioned interrogative (extract 2 line 13: "This is unbelievable.")
2. *Personal responsibility*: In the API, the IE tends to be presented as attempting to subvert the norms of the interview by evading the question (Harris, 1991). They might be left to dig a hole for themselves as the question is pursued. In the HPI, IEs are presented as personally responsible for holding/defending views that the IR personally takes issue with—in other words, even formalistic versions of journalistic neutralism can be

dispensed with at certain stages in the HPI (extract 2 lines 23–26: "N<u>ow</u> it's okay fer <u>fem</u>inists, .h tuh <u>ri</u>dicule women... <u>Go</u> for it Gloria.")

3. *Use of personal pro-terms*: In the HPI, not only may IEs be personally associated with a contentious issue/statement/position by the use of "you," but IRs will also readily use the pro-term "I" to personalize the argument being conducted within the interview; IRs will openly associate themselves with standpoints in opposition to that of the IE (extract 2 line 16's sarcastic "eHHH<u>HAAA</u>!=I <u>LOVE</u> it!" ((clap-clap))).

4. *Insults*: Unlike in the API, in the HPI, the IR may readily subject the IE to personal insult, whether through name calling ("You're a coward"; "You're the zealot"; "Your far left lunacy" (extracts to be shown below) or through negative association (extract 2 lines 19–20: "Ay <u>fem</u>inist is att<u>a</u>cking a woman for how she looks.")

5. *Emotional heightening*: In the API, emotional outbursts mainly come from IEs, who have been known to walk out of the interview; IRs typically remain calm, even when pursuing a question over numerous iterations. In the HPI, outbursts of emotion—especially anger—more readily occur, but this time involving the IR; certain IRs take the license to "go ballistic," especially when faced with what they perceive as lying, evasiveness or other moral reprehensibility on the part of IEs. While IEs may occasionally respond with their own anger, much more frequently the IE tends to present a passive response to the outburst, manifesting verbal or paraverbal signals of powerlessness in the face of the tirade.

GOING BALLISTIC

Of the numerous distinctive characteristics of the HPI in relation to the API, the one that is perhaps most significant, and certainly the feature that is most frequently picked up in social media commentary about the genre, is the last on the above list: emotionally heightened episodes of interaction, particularly those involving anger.

In conventional news interviewing, emotions are rarely shown, especially by the interviewer. In the Jeremy Paxman–Michael Howard interview analyzed at length in chapter 5, although Paxman's repetition of his question is emphatic and he is clearly frustrated by Howard's obfuscation, his demeanor remains controlled throughout and does not verge into heightened emotion such as anger and shouting.

In conventional news interviews, if heightened emotion does play a role it tends to be in the behavior of interviewees, who have been known to lose their temper with the line of questioning adopted by the interviewer, and even to walk out of the interview while on air. An example of the first type of case is extract (3), in which the businessman Sir James Goldsmith accuses the interviewer of misrepresenting him in a previous broadcast and demands, in a raised voice, to know why; while the interviewer calmly (and using explicit politeness markers; see line 11) requests that the interviewee observe the norms of the setting by allowing him to ask the questions:

```
(3)  (Greatbatch, 1988: 421-2)

1     IE:   despite the fact there were fou:r major factories
2           that you knew about,=despite the fact there was a two
3           hundred and thirty million capital investment programme
4           that you knew about,=.hhh that we dealt in companies you
5           stated and restated toda::y, .hhh despite the fact that
6           ninety one per cent of our companies are still there:,=
7           and only the marginal ones which you knew were sold, .hhh
8           and you e:ven mislead people by suggesting for instance
9           that we owned the Parisian publishing house Brooke.
10          Why.=
11    IR:   =s-s-s-Sir James I['m so sorry (        ) I'm so s-
12→   IE:                    [No,=I'm asking a question now.=
13    IR:   =It's more conventional in these programmes [fo:r
14→   IE:                                               [Well I
15→         don't mind ab[out     convention. = ]I'm asking you why
16    IR:                [me to ask questions,]
17          (.)
18→   IE:   you distorted those facts.
```

The following extract provides an example of the second type in which an outburst of anger from the interviewee is occasioned by a question put to him by Sir Robin Day, an early British exponent of the adversarial political interview:

```
(4)  TVN: Day-Nott

1     IR:   But why should the public on this issue:: .hh as
```

```
2            regards the future of the Royal Navy believe you=a
3            transient .hhh er here toda:y and .hh if I may say
4            so gone tomorro:w politician [rather than] a senior=
5    IE:                                 [(         )]
6    IR:  =officer of many years [experience,]
7→   IE:                         [I'm sorry ] I'm I'm fed up
8            with this interview really ((standing, removes
9            microphone from tie, throws it down and walks off
10           camera))
11   IR:  Thank you Mister Nott.
```

Here, cabinet minister John Nott is subject to an aggressive line of questioning from the interviewer. The extract shows a particularly insulting question, in which the minister is described as a "here toda:y and .hh if I may say so gone tomorro:w politician," to which he responds by angrily removing his clip-on microphone and withdrawing bodily from the studio. (Notice how in this case the politeness marker "if I may say so" has a distinct edge of sarcasm and indeed appears to heighten the *im*politeness of the question.)

In the HPI outbursts of emotion—especially anger—far more readily occur, and in this context they tend to involve the interviewer rather than the interviewee. As noted, certain HPI interviewers take the license to "go ballistic." In order to explore this aspect of the hybrid interview format, I will examine one particular example. Extract (5) below is from an interview that took place at the height of the 2008 financial crash, and concerned the role of politician Barney Frank, Chair of the House of Representatives Finance Committee, in regulating the two major US government-sponsored lending agencies known as Fannie Mae and Freddie Mac. The mortgage lending policies of these organizations played a major part in the buildup of "toxic debt" that underpinned the banking crisis, as (encouraged by legislation introduced under the Clinton administration and supported by the subsequent Bush administration) they lent large amounts to home buyers from the poorer sectors of society, who it turned out did not have the wherewithal to keep up their repayments. (A similar thing was happening in the de-mutualized ex-building society banking sector in the UK, albeit for different reasons.)

The interview is conducted via live two-way. In the studio the IR sits behind a medium-sized desk facing the camera; while on a screen embedded into the main televised image the IE sits in what looks like an official Washington office. The IE carries a sheaf of papers throughout, which he is seen looking through as he first comes into the shot as the first question is asked. The interview itself has been preceded by a video compilation of Frank's recent public statements in which he is heard to be denying that there is any major problem with Fannie Mae or Freddie Mac's finances. We then return to the studio:

```
(5) O'REILLY FACTOR: Banking crash

1    IR:   Joining us now from Washington i:::s Congressman
2          Frank, (0.3) .h A:nd uh we appreciate yuh comin' in,
3          bein' a standup guy=but shouldn't everybody in
4          the country be an:gry with you right now?
5          (0.5: IE RUSTLES PAPERS)
6    IE:   No::, you've misrepresented this consistently. I
7          became chairman of the committee o:n uh January
8          thirty first two thousan' and seven...
((Some lines omitted: History of Frank's regulatory initiatives))
9          ... so, .h the earliest chance I got to put tough
10         regulation tuh Fannie Mae and Freddie Mac, .h we did it.
11   IR:   Alright, that's swe:ll but, you still went ou:t in:-
12         July:: and said everything was grea:t, an' o:ff that
13         a lotta people bought sto::ck, and lost everything they
14         ha[:d.=A::nd- ↑y[e:s=↑Oh yes. .h [↑O:H, (0.2) ↓Y:ES:.
15   IE:      [Oh no.      [I sh-            [No I >said it wasn't
16         a good investment.<= Plea[se stop yelling.
17   IR:                             [Don't gimme any o' dat,
18         we just heard duh words..h [What're you a- what're
19   IE:                              [(Look let's talk-
20   IR:   =you- [dat-you= didn' say dat? Y'want me da play it=
21   IE:        [Look let's talk rationally:,
22   IR:   =again for ya?
23   IE:   Yuh- You didn't listen to it. [The (yet ee- u-)
24   IR:                                 [No. .h I listened to
```

```
25              every word yuh [sai:d, .h And I ['ave the tra:nscript
26    IE:                      [u-no uh-         [no y-
27    IR:    =right [here.
28    IE:           [en I said it wasn't ay good investment.
29    IR:    Yeah. [And you said going forward we're gunna=
30    IE:          [I said it wasn't a-
31    IR:    =be SWELL..h f'r=Look. [Fr'm August oh seventh=
32    IE:                           [No, I didn't say swell.
33    IE:    =tuh [August oh eighth,
34    IR:         [Excuse me, Bill,
35    IR:    Doh-=doh-=look. Stop the BEE ESS here. .h
36           STO:[P the CRA:P. .hh [from August oh seven tuh]=
37    IE:        [E:r (  )         [Y'know,y'know the problem]=
38    IR:    =[August oh eighth, UNder YOUR TUTELAGE, .h THIS=
39    IE:    =[with going- Y'know here's the problem going on=
40    IR:    =[this industry, declined ninety percent.
41    IE:    =[your show.
42    IR:    .h NINE[ty percent.
43    IE:           [Yes but it-
44           (.)
45    IR:    hOh. [.h None o' this    was yo:ur fau:lt.
46    IE:         [Now do I get a chance tuh talk?
47    IR:    .h ↑OH NO..h People lo[st MILLions uh dollars,
48    IE:                          [Do I get a chance tuh talk?
49    IR:    It WASN'T YOUR= fau:lt. .h Come on you coward.
50           .hh ↑SAY the [TRUTH.
51    IE:                 [Whaddaya mean coward.
52    IR:    [[You're a coward. Yuh blame everybody else.
53    IE:    [[Do I get a chance tuh talk? May I talk?
54    IR:    .hh You're a coward.
```

As noted, this interview begins with a fairly conventional pre-interview sequence in which the IR, having introduced the issue, plays a videotape of previous statements made by the upcoming IE (these data are not shown). As this extract begins, the IR then introduces the IE, following which there is an initial question-answer sequence as part of which Frank gets to produce a lengthy account of his role in the Fannie Mae-Freddie Mac affair. Then, somewhat abruptly, in the IR's turn in lines 11–14, there is a noticeable shift in the tenor of the interview into an emotionally heightened mode. It seems that, having heard the IE disagree with his statement (note the "<u>O</u>h no" in line 15) the IR "goes ballistic." This shift happens quickly, and for the rest of the extract we remain in the mode of what seems like an increasingly angry, increasingly argumentative and accusatory, interchange. In the following analysis, I consider the details of how this shift from "interview" to "argument" is managed in the turn-by-turn unfolding of the talk.

FROM INTERVIEW TO ARGUMENT

The first question is particularly important in this interview as it represents the slot in which the IR seeks to relate the pre-recorded video materials to the IE who is now seen in co-presence by the audience: in other words, selected elements of previous happenings and statements are brought into the immediate interactional present and made accountable in the here and now. In the construction of first questions we can find an important similarity between the API and the HPI, namely the use of *assertoric* questions. Montgomery (2007: 214) states that in some accountability interviews, "the structure of questions and answers is replaced by assertion and counter-assertion." He gives examples such as the following, from the British mainstream Channel 4 News broadcast:

```
(6)  (Montgomery, 2007:215)

1    IR:    Zvi Ravner who's the:: er Deputy Israeli Ambassador to London
2           he joins us now (.) (hh) Zvi Ravner (.) this is collective
3           punishment (.) you've cut off the water you've cut off the
4           petrol you've cut off the electricity (.) and you're starving
5           the hospitals out
6    IE:    (this is) not a:: collective punishment...
```

Here, the IR's first turn takes the form of an assertion ("this is collective punishment") followed by statements that provide the grounds for that assertion. The IE responds by countering that assertion (line 6).

However, the use of assertoric questions does not always entail shifting away from the norms of interviewing by *replacing* the first question with an assertion. Note that, in the above extract, the assertion could have been worded as a question ("Isn't this collective punishment?"), hence preserving those norms. In a slightly different sense, HPI interviewers frequently produce initial moves that are structured as questions but that imply tendentious assertions.

For example, in extract (5), the IR's turn in lines 3–4, "shouldn't everyone in the country be angry with you right now?" is grammatically formed as a question; however, it strongly implies an assertion: "Everyone in the country *should be* angry with you right now." A differently structured example of the same type is shown below, drawn from another HPI:

```
(7) O'REILLY FACTOR: Military recruiters

1     IR:    joining us now from San Francisco, .h civil rights
2            attorney, .h Angela Alioto. .hh Angela, m-uh, gonna go
3→           right to this one, OK? Why[::, are you all afrai:d of=
4     IE:                              [Absolutely.
5→    IR:    =military recruiters in our schools? Why are
6            you af[raid of military recruiters?
6     IE:          [Um,
7            (.)
8     IE:    I- I- I don't think the word afraid is u::h uh:
9            relevan[t.=I (                          )
10    IR:           [Petrified. How 'bout=How 'bout petrified.
```

Again, the question "*Why are* you afraid of military recruiters?" implies the assertion (and indeed, the accusation), "*You are* afraid of military recruiters."

The loaded nature of such questions places the IE in the position of deciding how to respond, not just to the question, but to the implicit assertion. In extract (7), as we see, the IE attempts to deny the relevance of the accusatory word chosen by the IR ("afraid"). In sequential terms this turns out to provide a resource by which the IR elects not to withdraw, but to *upgrade* the implicit accusation. Overlapping the IE's continuation of her turn, the IR substitutes the stronger term "petrified." She thus treats the denial of the relevance of "afraid" not as a challenge to the implied assertion, but as requiring that the assertion itself should be intensified.

However, not all IE responses to assertoric IR questions result in such third-position rejoinders. In our target extract (5), the IE chooses to disagree with the implied assertion ("No::, you've misrepresented this consistently"). He is then granted extended floor space to produce a long turn in which he defends his stance, outlining an alternative narrative supported by a number of factual and historical statements (not shown above).

It is in the sequence following this, from line 11 onwards, that we can observe the emergence of what might be called the hybrid pivot in this interview: the moment at which the speech exchange system itself—the norms of turn-taking to which the participants are observably oriented—shifts from that of adversarial news interview to that of confrontational argument.

In lines 11–14, the IR begins on an assertoric turn which implies that, on the basis of the IE's recommendations regarding Fannie Mae and Freddie Mac, people who bought stock "lost everything they ha:d." He then indicates that he seeks to hold the floor to produce a next turn component, with a latched, and emphasized, "A::nd." However, in line 15, the IE overlaps that floorholding move with "Oh no."

```
(5) Detail

11    IR:    Alright, that's swe:ll but, you still went ou:t in:-
12           July:: and said everything was grea:t, an' o:ff that
13           a lotta people bought sto::ck, and lost everything they
14→          ha[:d.=A::nd-
15→   IE:       [Oh no.
```

Now here, in terms of the turn-taking system for interviews, the IE may be treated as interrupting a question-preface in progress. It is not clear, as he begins to speak, whether or not the IR is in fact going to complete his current turn subsequently by asking a question. In other words, the IE is at least hearable as breaching the norm that IEs should refrain from speaking until a question has been asked. However, in terms of the turn-taking system for *conversation*, there is a clear warrant for him starting up at that point, in that the IR's claim that he said "everything was great" (line 12) counts as an accusation, given the banking crash that ensued. A strong conversational preference is for accusations to be denied at the earliest sequential opportunity, which is what the IE attempts to do in line 15.

However that might be, what is significant is the way the IR abandons any next clause presaged by the floor holding "A::nd," instead shifting to a direct, and increasingly emotionally heightened, series of contradictions of Frank's denial: "↑ye:s=↑Oh yes. .h ↑O:H, (0.2) ↓Y:ES:."

It is at this point that the interview becomes truly hybrid. I remarked earlier that the HPI combines structural features of the news interview with other speech exchange systems, including conversational argument formats. From line 14 onward, we observe the IR progressively moving away from the norms of interviewer conduct (restricting oneself to asking questions which elicit the viewpoint of the interviewee), while the IE responds initially by seeking to argue his point (lines 15–16), then by orienting toward the breach of interview norms (line 21):

```
(5) Detail

11    IR:    Alright, that's swe:ll but, you still went ou:t in:-
12           July:: and said everything was grea:t, an' o:ff that
13           a lotta people bought sto::ck, and lost everything they
14→          ha[:d.=A::nd-  ↑y[e:s=↑Oh yes. .h [↑O:H, (0.2) ↓Y:ES:.
15    IE:    [Oh no.       [I sh-           [No I >said it wasn't
16           a good investment.<= Plea[se stop yelling.
17    IR:                             [Don't gimme any o' dat,
18           we just heard duh words..h [What're you a- what're
19    IE:                                [(Look let's talk-
20    IR:    =you- [dat-you didn' say dat? Y'want me da play it=
21→   IE:          [Look let's talk rationally:,
22    IR:    =again for ya?
```

In this detail we see from the IR a series of belligerent statements ("Don't gimme any o' dat, we just heard duh words") and rhetorical questions, accompanied paraverbally by a shift into a pugnacious, hearably colloquial mode of pronunciation in contrast to his earlier, more measured journalistic register ("You didn't say dat? Yuh want me duh play it again for ya?"). The IE produces turns in overlap with this that orient both to the manner of delivery, that is, the emotional heightening itself ("Please stop yelling"), and to a perceived move away from rational discussion ("let's talk rationally").

A further moment where these markers of hybridity are shown with particular clarity can be highlighted. Once again, both the doing of non-neutrality, and the marking of this as a hybrid exchange somewhere between interview and argument, are observable in the emotionally heightened enunciation of the IR's evaluation of the IE's conduct (lines 35–36):

```
(5) Detail

35    IR:    Doh-=doh-=look. Stop the BEE ESS here. .h
36           STO:[P the CRA:P.
```

As Clayman and Heritage (2002: 31) point out, British exponent of the API Jeremy Paxman once suggested that the question "Why is this lying bastard lying to me?" (originally attributed to *Times* reporter Louis Heren) represents "a sound principle from which to operate" as a political news interviewer. However, one of the differences between the API and the HPI is that in the former, while the interviewer may carry that assumption, he or she does not overtly state the accusation. In the HPI, as above, the interviewer has no compunction in stating that the interviewee is peddling "BEE ESS" and "CRA:P." Thus, even formalistic neutralism is dispensed with entirely.

More aspects of non-neutrality in this particular interview are mentioned in later pages. For now, I want to turn to two other sequential devices commonly used in the HPI to index a move between interview and argument: first, polar contrastives; and then the use of pronouns and derogatory personalization.

CONTRASTIVES

Other explicit moves into the territory of outright argument in the HPI involve the use of polar contrastives (Yes/No, It is/It is not, etc.) to disagree overtly with the interlocutor. Extract (8) is taken from an interview in which feminist blogger Joan Walsh is speaking in defense of the head of an abortion clinic who has been murdered by anti-abortion activists. Previously the IR has suggested that while the clinic operated legally, its practices were morally wrong. We see the use of a polar contrastive ("No") by the IR to deny the IE's attempt to establish a particular line of discussion as the interview proceeds:

```
(8) O'REILLY FACTOR: Abortion clinic

1    IE:    ...there're a lot of things that are legal in this
2           country that, people are very upset about. .hh Ther:e
3           are people who think guns should be abolishe[d.=I'm=
4    IR:                                                [Oh yeah.
```

```
5      IE:    =not one of them but let's just take th[at as an example.
6→     IR:                                           [No, we're not
7             gunna take that as an example.
```

The polar contrastive is found in line 6 as the IR responds by seeking to deny the IE's attempt to control the topic. Although this is begun in overlap, it is at a place which Jefferson (1986) described as "recognitional onset" —that is, the general gist of the IE's turn is discernible at that point. Hence, while only partially interruptive (where full interruption involves deeper incursions into ongoing turns than recognitional onset), the turn nevertheless issues a direct dismissal of the IE's attempted line of talk.

It is worth observing what takes place as this interview proceeds further. As we see in the following extract, not only does the IR continue to argue against the position being developed by the IE, but the IE herself plays a large part in the construction of an argumentative frame:

```
(9) O'REILLY FACTOR: Abortion clinic
1      IE:    ...there're a lot of things that are legal in this
2             country that, people are very upset about. .hh Ther:e
3             are people who think guns should be abolishe[d.=I'm=
4      IR:                                                [Oh yeah.
5      IE:    =not one of them but let's just take th[at as an example.
6      IR:                                           [No, we're not
7             gunna take [that as an example. [We have more important]=
8      IE:               [Oka::y?             [Now would it be oka:y ]=
9      IR:    =[things to talk about than fear'v-
10     IE:    =[fer those people,.h to go crusade against gun dealers
11            and put their pictures up and call them BABY killers,
12            .h and say they have b:LOOD on their hand[s, .h and-=
13     IR:                                             [Look.
14     IE:    =.p .t picket their [sto:res.=That's a legal that's a=
15     IR:                        [Joan look you can- c'n make
16     IE:    =that's a legal right, [.h that many people think, should=
17     IR:                           [any theoretical argument you want.
```

```
18   IE:    =not be. .h[h You need tuh change the la:ws, .h you=
19   IR:              [Joan.
20   IE:    =don't need to crusade like a vigilante, against
21          some[one performing a legal, medical, procedure.
22   IR:        [O:h, baloney.
23   IE:    [[And that's what you did.
24→  IR:    [[I didn't crusade anything.=Everything I reported is
25→         absolutely tru:e. .hh Tiller, (.) was running, an
26          abortion mill::,
```

In line 8, as the IR continues with his refusal of the IE's proposed line about gun control ("We have more important things to talk about . . ."), the IE begins on a continuation of her previous turn and continues in overlap until, in line 10, she finally gains clear turn-space. At this point she begins to build an argument referring to earlier reports in which the IR had controversially referred to the clinic head as "a baby killer," describing his (IR's) actions as "crusad[ing] like a vigilante," and finally personalizing this criticism, and implying complicity in the death of Dr. Tiller, with "And that's what you did" (line 23).

At various points in this turn, the IR makes attempts to issue rejoinders; in line 13, "Look," then in line 15 "Joan look . . ." and in line 19, "Joan." In each case, the IE retains the floor by building a next increment onto her turn, marked through inbreaths, conjunctions and latching:

line 12, hand[s .h and- .p .t picket
line 14, [sto:res.=That's a legal
line 18, should not be.=.h[h=You need tuh change the la:ws

What we see here are typical markers of an argument frame: implied or explicit personal criticism, attempts to issue rejoinders or rebuttals, maintenance of the floor by continuing with a turn in overlap, hence treating the interlocutor's turns as interruptive (Hutchby, 1992, 2008). Notably, it is not just the IR but the IE who plays a key role in this. In fact, it is at the point where the IE "goes personal" using the insulting phrase "crusade like a vigilante" that the IR retakes the offensive, using the contrastive phrase "O:h baloney I didn't crusade anything.=Everything I reported is absolutely tru:e." Again, we find elements in the IR's talk that go beyond the normative bounds of the news interview: the use of (mild) cursing, the use of the first-person

134   *Chapter Seven*

reference to the IR's own activities, and the assertion not just of objectivity or neutrality in previous reports, but of their absolute truth.

Polar contrastives are also used by the IR to respond to IE turns in which there is some disagreement with a declarative statement on the IR's part. Consider the following extract:

```
(10)  O'REILLY FACTOR: Abortion clinic
 1    IR:   So- so yihknow, a-a woman with breast cancer, who, .hh was
 2          g-u:h undergoing chemo or whatever couldn't (.) have gotten
 3          the abortion unless she could come up with six thousand
 4          bucks. .hh He wasn't doin' it pro [bono.
 5→   IE:                                    [That wasn't always true
 6          a:c[tually.
 7→   IR:      [Yes it was. It was ac[tually- It was actually almost a=
 8    IE:                            [He actually did (      )
 9    IR:   =hundred percent true. .h Because you haven't [seen-
10    IE:                                                 [re- really-
11    IR:   Miss Walsh, have you seen [the investigative documents?
12    IE:                             [Bill, we-we just have- we have
13          different- we have different st[udies  an'  we  have=
14→   IR:                                  [No, yihknow, it isn't=
15    IE:   =[different sets of facts on this (      ).
16    IR:   =[a matter of difference. It's a matter of facts.
```

In line 5, the IE states that the claim that only women who could afford "six bucks" were able to use the abortion clinic is not true. The IR responds to this disagreement by issuing a blunt polar contrastive, "Yes it was" (line 7), subsequently bolstering it using the slightly strange phrase, "It was actually almost a hundred percent true."

The extract subsequently develops along the lines of one of the common tropes of aggravated dispute: a "competency challenge" in which each speaker's competence to comment on a given issue is challenged by the other (Goodwin, 1990; Maynard, 1985; Hutchby, 1996). In the course of this, the IR begins to suggest that IE's competency may be compromised because she has not seen "investigative documents" on the case (line 9), before re-phrasing this turn as a question (line 11). The IE meanwhile asserts that they each give credence to "different sets of facts" (line 15). At this point, momentarily abandoning his line about investigative documents, the IR resorts to another polar contrastive, in lines 14–16, "No . . . it isn't a <u>mat</u>ter of difference. It's a matter of <u>fact</u>s."

PERSONALIZATION

The above discussion also begins to indicate the role of personalization in the argument frame, including insulting the interlocutor, assigning personal responsibility, attributing beliefs or motives, and position taking. While both IR and IE can engage in these activities, they particularly go against the conventions of IR conduct such as the neutralistic injunctions not to take up stances or engage in personal attacks on the IE. The HPI abounds with examples of personalization.

Extract (11) shows how the IR, receiving what he evidently takes to be an unsatisfactory response to a question, can quickly proceed to personalization, in this case bringing up alleged accusations that the IE has previously directed at him:

```
(11)   O'REILLY FACTOR: Abortion clinic

1      IR:    .h Have you seen the investigative documents the state
2             of Kansas put together against Tiller. .h=Have you madam?
3→     IE:    I: have skimmed them.
4→     IR:    You have s::KIMmed th[em.
5      IE:                         [I have skimmed-[I have skimmed th'm]=
6      IR:                                         [You have-=then you ]=
7      IE:    =[yes=I have skimmed them.
8      IR:    =[kno- Well if you have skimmed them=an' it's .hh
9      IR:    it's .hh shocking to me that you wouldn't read them,
10            .h if you're gunna accuse somebody like me: of being
11            a vi:le accomplice to murder, .h that you wouldn't
12            read them, bu[t if you skimmed them, if you skimmed them,]=
13     IE:                 [I didn't accuse you- I said you were vile.]=
```

```
14   IR:   =[did you s-
15   IE:   =[I did. I did not accuse you, of being an accomplice to
16         murder so let's b[e really clear, .hh [about our=
17   IR:                   [A' right.              [Fine.
18   IE:   =language here [Bill. I never said it.
19   IR:                  [I'm vi::le because, I'm looking out.
20         for, (.) late term fetuses who you believe have no rights
21         at a:ll
```

In this extract, the competency challenge segment that began in extract (10) above continues with the IR's question in lines 1–2. Following on from the originally abandoned statement "Because you haven't seen," this question is based on the IR's evident suspicion that IE has not read "investigative documents" which he himself claims to have read. Considered in this light, the IE's answer, "I: have skimmed them," provides him with perfect evidence to press home the competency challenge. To have *skimmed* documents, as marked by the IR's emphatic rejoinder in line 4 (and again in lines 8–9 where he contrasts having "skimmed" with having "read" the documents), is to have given them only cursory attention and hence to be less than competent to comment on the relevant issue.

It is in the course of the following exchange that we find the discourse becoming personalized, primarily through the use of two further resources that move outside the interview frame: position attribution and personal insult. First, IR criticizes the IE for "accus[ing] somebody like me: of being a vi:le accomplice to murder" (lines 10–11). IE then starts up in overlap to deny this, or at least to qualify it ("I said you were vile. I did. I did not accuse you, of being an accomplice to murder"). In the first part of this qualification, the IE clearly lets the personal insult 'vile' stand. The IR responds by producing an ironic account for the IE's use of this insulting term, which involves position taking and the attribution of motives and beliefs. The reason she treats him as vile, he claims, is that he is "looking out. for, (.) late term fetuses." In other words, quite apart from his present role as a news journalist, he is acting in the interests of a particular constituency; moreover, one that cannot speak for itself. The IR thus takes up a position. Having done so, he then attributes a contrasting position to the IE. Although she has not stated as much previously during the interview, he assigns to her the belief that "late term fetuses" have "no rights at a:ll" (lines 20–21).

Irony, sarcasm and personal insult also play a major part in the following extract:

(12) O'REILLY FACTOR: Banking crash

```
41   IR:   hOh. [.h None o' this was yo:ur fau:lt. .h ↑OH NO.
42   IE:        [Now do I get a chance tuh talk?
43   IR:   .h People lo[st MILLions uh dollars, it WASN'T YOUR=
44   IE:               [Do I get a chance tuh talk?
45   IR:   =fau:lt. .h Come on you coward. .hh ↑SAY the [TRUTH.
46   IE:                                                [Whaddaya
47   IE:   mean coward.
48   IR:   [[You're a coward. Yuh blame everybody else.
49   IE:   [[Do I get a chance tuh talk? May I talk?
50   IR:   .hh You're a coward.
```

Here, we see the IR launching more directly into an attack on the IE's personal character. The turn in line 41 begins with "Oh," a component that is often used in argumentative environments to preface disputatiously ironic moves (Hutchby, 2001b). In the rest of the turn, the IR sarcastically implies that despite IE's objections, it was his fault that "people lost MILLions uh dollars" during the financial crash. He then moves more deeply into the terrain of personal insult by calling the IE a "coward" and implying (with "SAY the TRUTH") that he is also a liar.

At this point, we again find the IE shifting between orientation to interview vs. conversational rules of exchange; occasioned this time by the striking move deep into the discourse of personalized attack by the IR in line 45. From merely attempting to play his part as an interviewee with turns such as "Do I get a chance tuh talk?" the IE, at the point where IR moves perhaps furthest from the neutralistic stance of the interviewer ('Come on you coward'), shifts momentarily into the conversational argument frame (line 46): "Whaddaya mean coward." In terms of the interview's hybrid format, therefore, here is a moment in which the rules of exchange for ordinary argument—not only sequentially, but in terms of the unmitigated use of personal attack—completely supplant those of the news interview.

The final example shows a more extended sequence in which both IR and IE adopt an argumentative frame using personalization. The maintenance of an argument frame is also marked by the consistent use of overlapping and interruptive talk (Hutchby, 1992).

(13) O'REILLY FACTOR: Abortion clinic

```
1→   IE:   =Twenny four time[s you called 'im a baby killer.
2    IR:                [Over   a   period,   of   fi::ve
3          yea:rs,h he was [running an abortion mi:ll,
4    IE:                           [Four.
5    IR:   Ev'rybody in Kansas=kn[ows it,
6    IE:                         [A legal, [facility.
7→   IR:                                   [and you don't care.
8          .h You, don'[t, (.) ca:re.
9    IE:               [He was running a legal [facility.
10   IR:                                       [Yihknow who
11→        'as blood on their hands? YOU. .hh Y:OU don't
12         car[e about these babies,
13   IE:      [That's ridiculous Bil[l,
14   IR:                            [Id ISn' ridiculous.
15→        .h=YOU're the zealo[t.
16   IE:                      [Yihknow you're [really-
17→  IR:                                      [You::'re the
18         zealot.=
19→IE:    =You're a piece a' work=m[y friend.
20   IR:                           [No you're the one who
21         has bl[ood on their hands.
22→  IE:         [.h I don't have blood on my ha[:nds, you do.
23→  IR:                                        [You::'re the zealot,
```

In the first part of the extract (lines 1–9) there is an exchange of position attribution and position taking. With the topic being Dr. Tiller, the murdered abortion clinic chief, IE attributes to IR the extreme position that Tiller was "a baby killer" (line 1); this statement in itself implies a move into social advocacy (anti-abortionism) on the IR's part. The IR counters not by disavowing this advocacy, but by reformulating it in a position-taking statement that

Tiller was "running an abortion mi:ll." He uses an extreme case formulation (Pomerantz, 1986) to bolster this stance ("Ev'rybody in Kansas knows it"); and while the IE attempts to argue a counter-position (the clinic was "a legal facility") IR continues with another position attribution directed toward the IE, "you don't care."

The second part of the extract sees both participants moving into the territory of personal insult. Particularly noticeable here is the use of personal pronouns (primarily "you" but also "I") to target the insults directly at the speaker's co-present interlocutor.

From line 10, the IR, maintaining a markedly non-neutral and indeed belligerent stance, issues a series of declarative turns that castigate the IE in strong terms. Each of these prominently features the pro-term *you*:

Yihknow who 'as blood on their hands? YOU.
Y:OU don't care about these babies.
YOU're the zealot.

In response, IE produces her own closely matched rejoinders:

You're a piece a' work.
I don't have blood on my ha:nds, you do.

This sequence of turns displays the features of what Goodwin (1990) called "aggravated opposition." As can be seen at various junctures in the present analysis, degrees of opposition, confrontation, disagreement and so on can vary in the course of an argument. The variation ranges from mitigated formats in which disagreements may be prefaced by phrases such as "Yes, but" or "Alright, that's swell, but" to aggravated formats in which oppositional turns are constructed precisely in order to highlight rather than downplay their oppositional character. We saw above that the transition between mitigated and aggravated variants of opposition can take place rapidly, as the IR moves from a mitigated disagreement in "that's swell, but" to an aggravated format with "↑ye:s=↑Oh yes. .h ↑O:H, (0.2) ↓Y:ES:" in the course of one exchange of turns. In a similar sense, the sequence of insults and position-attributions described above are constructed so as to downplay politeness markers and highlight their personal character. The bandying back and forth of unmitigated, lexically matched, pro-termed declarative utterances heightens the degree to which the interview has not simply hybridized, but transmogrified into an argument.

CONCLUSION

Personalization is an issue that has been given considerable attention over the past few years in studies of news interview discourse (Clayman, 2010; Lauerbach, 2010; Montgomery, 2010; Thornborrow, 2010). In these studies, one of the central themes is the way that personal matters, personal feelings or experiences are brought into play in the expressly public sphere of the television interview. For example, Clayman (2010) shows how the use of personal pro-terms by interviewees is often bound up with managing expressive or heartfelt properties of talk, or disjunctive (topic-shifting or disagreeing) turns in conventional news interviews.

In the HPI, by contrast, the kinds of personalization described in this chapter—personal insults, direct position attributions and so on—are bound up with more extreme forms of disagreement. Turns and turn-components such as these, produced in the overall context of belligerent and argumentative exchanges on socially controversial topics, contribute to a further level of personalization in the public domain of media talk, emphasizing the shift into hybridity and away from neutrality. In this sense, we can perhaps think of a continuum along which personalization functions in the evolution of broadcast news talk, from the increasing use of personal experience to contextualize major events, which itself evolves out of the original *vox populi* formats of early broadcasting (Corner, 1991), to the use of conversational insult formulations to highlight the argumentative nature of a hybrid interview.

Another of the key features of the HPI highlighted through the preceding analysis has been that of non-neutrality. Rather than adopting the conventional stance of the news interviewer, seeking to elicit information and viewpoints from interviewees without overtly expressing them on one's own behalf, in the HPI the interviewer readily takes up stances, disagrees with interviewees, and crucially, seeks to speak for certain sectors of the population. A key question thus becomes, does this tendency extend beyond the opinionated types of broadcast in which the HPI emerged, into other more mainstream types of political interview? That is one of the questions that we turn to in the remainder of this book.

Chapter Eight

Tribuneship, Objectivity, and the Public Interest

In this chapter, I want to explore one last arena of language use in which the interview's strategic interaction "game" (Heritage and Clayman, 2002) is played out: tribuneship, or the matter of who speaks "for the people." Both politicians, as elected representatives supposedly acting in the public interest, and news journalists, as self-appointed guardians holding politicians to account in the interests of the public, can be said to be attempting to speak for the people. However, as this chapter will show, in the increasingly non-neutral environment of the contemporary political interview, this issue quickly becomes one of who, in fact, "the people" are, which "people" we are talking about, and who has the power ultimately to delineate which sector of "the people" are being addressed in any given question-answer exchange.

TRIBUNESHIP

In the ancient Roman constitution, the tribuneship was an elected office with responsibility for protecting the interests of the plebeians in the patrician senate. Later, as newspaper journalism developed in the nineteenth and twentieth centuries, many newspapers adopted the name *Tribune* to convey a sense that they reported news in the interests of the ordinary people, as opposed to those of government or business. As suggested above, the term tribuneship is used here to refer to the ways in which interviewers can display, in the design and content of their questioning, an orientation toward their journalistic role as one of speaking for or representing the interests of ordinary people. It is also a role through which adversarial interviewers tend to justify their asking of tough questions (Clayman, 2002). Lastly, in this adopted role of tribune, they can equally be challenged to varying degrees by interviewees.

In many types of news interview, particularly adversarial and accountability interviews, IRs orient to their own self-presentation as representing the public interest, looking out for the underrepresented, seeking the truth, and so on. One of the main ways of doing this is for the IR to invoke the listening public as stakeholders, either directly or indirectly (as in "people listening to this will want to know . . .").

For example, in extract (1) the participants are involved in a discussion about the proposal that British Muslims who emigrate to join the fundamentalist group Islamic State should be banned from returning to Britain and be stripped of their citizenship:

```
(1) Daily Politics: Neil-Thornberry

1      IE:   We had earlier (.) a discussion about the importance of
2            international la::w,=about putting people up for trial
3            you cannot pick and choo:se, .h [which of those we want.
4→     IR:                                   [Well actually most people
5→           watching this programme, .h will be less concerned about
6→           international law and more concerned that these people
7            who've beheaded, .h fellow American and British
8            citizen:s,.h a:re, .h are gonna come back and do us harm.
```

In lines 1–3, the IE is putting forward the view that to strip such individuals' citizenship would be to render them stateless and so would be in breach of international law, as well as basic human rights legislation. She is arguing for the role of independent courts of law in adjudicating in such cases.

The IR begins his turn in line 4 as a rejoinder, rather than, as in the conventional interview framework, a next question or formulation. He goes on to make a statement that implies, or at least articulates a fear, that "these people," having "beheaded" ordinary citizens, "are gonna come back and do us harm." However, that statement is embedded within a kind of footing shift, in which authorship of that viewpoint is redistributed to "most people watching this program."

As Montgomery (2007: 179) puts it, in such instances interviewers move beyond conventional neutralism "into a more populist stance in which interviewers—like tribunes of the people—ventriloquize on behalf of a presumed skeptical public." This sense of ventriloquizing, or speaking for a presumed public interest, lends this type of tribuneship a degree of neutralism. With his shift in footing, the IR ventriloquizes in such a way as to be adversarial, even oppositional, while being seen to retain the professional journalistic standards of objectivity; avoiding the direct personal avowal of a position by attributing it instead to a watching, engaged, and in this instance, fearful "people."

Tribuneship can also be part of a more direct process in which the IR *foregrounds* his or her agency, spokespersonship, or expression of opinion in opposition to that of the interviewee. In HPI contexts, in particular, the IR tends not to ventriloquize on behalf of a generalized viewing public; rather he or she constructs situationally specific *sectoral* interests to represent, or more strictly to invoke, in the course of disputing with the IE.

In the following extract we find an example that is in some ways close to the conventional practice of invoking the public indirectly as stakeholders in the interview as pursuit of truth. However, that invocation of the skeptical public is placed within an overtly subjective evaluative framework:

```
(2)  O'REILLY FACTOR: Banking crisis

1    IE:   The pro:blem was, that- we pa:ssed in nineteen ninety

2          four in fact, [the bill, (tuh take-)

3    IR:                 [Yeah, now we're back to nineteen ninety

4          fou:r.

5    IE:   Yes [we are because-

6→   IR:       [This  is   bu::ll. .h [This is why Americans=

7    IE:                                [I'm (              )

8    IR:   =don't trust the government.

9    IE:   No:: this is where your stupidity gets in the

10         way of rational discussion. .h The fact is...
```

In line 6, the invocation of "Americans" is preceded by an explicit and subjective evaluation of the IE's talk: "This is bu::ll." Thus, although the IR as tribune can speak for "Americans" who "don't trust the government," that spokespersonship is placed inside a framework of personal stance-taking involving insult. In typical HPI fashion, that personal stance is stated in bare unmitigated terms: "bu::ll." Note that the IE in this particular case returns the insult: "No this is where your stupidity gets in the way of rational discussion," thereby colluding momentarily in the interview's hybrid format.

In extract (3) we see the IR acting as advocate for "a lotta people" who "lost everything they ha:d" during the 2008 financial crash (lines 7–8), but then invoking a wider listening public to which he himself belongs, but which is at least implicitly situated in opposition to the IE: "we" just heard [your] words (lines 11–12):

(3) O'REILLY FACTOR: Banking crisis

```
1    IE:   January of two thousan' n'eight, .h I asked Secretary
2          Paulson to put in the stimulus bill= so, .h the earliest
3          chance I got to put tough regulation tuh Fannie Mae and
4          Freddie Mac, .h we did it.
5    IR:   Alright, that's swe:ll but, you still went ou:t in:-
6          July:: and said everything was grea:t, an' o:ff that
7→         a lotta people bought sto::ck, and lost everything they
8          ha[:d.=A::nd- ↑y[e:s=↑Oh yes. .h [↑O:H, (0.2) ↓Y:ES:.
9    IE:      [Oh no.       [I sh-          [No I >said it wasn't
10         a good investment.<= Plea[se stop yelling.
11→  IR:                            [Don't gimme any o' dat, we just
12→        heard duh words.
```

In fact, as we can see, it is not just that the IR's use of the term "we" in the last two lines functions to align the IR himself with the presumed skeptical public in whose interests he proposes to be speaking. In the IE's preceding turn, he had constructed his own membership group, using the term "we" (line 4). Except that here, in "we did it," the IE invokes the government, possibly in order to bolster his own prior references, in lines 1 and 3, to himself in the first person. The problem is that not just the IE, but the government as a whole, is the object of the IR's critical line of questioning in this interview. Thus, the "we" for whom the IR seeks to speak becomes more readily identifiable as a group set up in opposition to the IE's line.

The following extract similarly shows the IR speaking *for* a particular group in society, but also doing alignment work involving both herself and the IE (a civil rights lawyer). The subject here is the placing of military recruitment materials in schools. The IR's line of questioning has sought to establish that the IE's opposition to this practice is politically motivated, primarily on the grounds that the IE's organization does not similarly object to the placing of what the IR calls left-wing materials in schools.

(4) O'REILLY FACTOR: Military recruiters

```
1    IE:   The question at stake here in Chicago, .h an' other
2          major mil- u::h major:, uh United States cities,
3          .h is whether or not, we are gunna have it inside,
```

```
4              the schools themselves. .h An- and in Chicago, .h they
5              were actually giving away the information (of) our
6              childre[n. (.) .hh which is just-
7    IR:             [Ri:ght. Yihknow what=yihknow what Christian,
8→             yihknow what Christian: people think across the
9→             country, especially .h yihknow pro-family groups?
10→            .h=They're really sick of, of fa:r le:ft. groups,
11→            coming into schools, .h a:nd putting their materials
12             out, but they always lo:se. in federal court=they
13             always lose,=.h=an' they're tol:d, .h to suck it up.=
14   IE:       =No.=
15   IR:       =That they ha[ve to they have to] agree:: with=
16   IE:                    [I:'m sorry Laura:,]
17   IR:       =the more progressive viewpoint.
```

In this instance, tribuneship is indexed by means of a rhetorical question, "yihknow what Chris:tian: people think ... especially ... pro-family groups?" The fact that this question is phrased declaratively, rather than in the interrogative form "*Do* you know what Christian people think?" serves both to construct it *as* rhetorical, and to distribute alignments between the IE and IR. The phrasing suggests that the IR possesses her own knowledge of the answer; thus, by knowing "what Christian people think," the IR at least implicitly aligns herself with the categories of Christians and pro-family groups. Correspondingly, the wording of the question suggests that the IE does *not* know "what Christian people think," and is therefore distanced from these groups. Moreover, the rest of the IR's turn in which she produces the answer to this rhetorical question shows her casting Christian and pro-family groups in a sympathetic light: their complaints about far left groups are dismissed and they are told "to suck it up." The IR here speaks for a particular sectoral interest within the wider social structure; and by aligning herself with that sector, she attempts to position the IE negatively in alignment with its implied opposite: "non-Christian" and "anti-family" groups.

In extract (5) we see another example of this kind of sectoral representation, this time in a more extreme form. The topic here is a recent spate of demonstrations and bomb attacks by pro-life activists at a Kansas abortion clinic, culminating in the shooting of its chief clinician, Dr. Tiller. Previously the IR has pressed the IE (a supporter of the clinic's activities) on whether she believes late-term fetuses should have human rights that protect them from abortion. The IE having evaded this question, the interview then turns to critical comments that the IE is reported as having posted about the IR on her website:

```
(5) O'REILLY FACTOR: Abortion clinic
 1   IR:  it's .hh shocking to me that you wouldn't read them,
 2        .h if you're gunna accuse somebody like me: of being
 3        a vi:le accomplice to murder, .h that you wouldn't
 4        read them, bu[t if you skimmed them, if you skimmed them,
 5   IE:               [I didn't accuse you-  I said you were vile.=
 6   IR:  =[did you s-
 7   IE:   [I did. I did not accuse you, of being an accomplice to
 8        murder so let's b[e really clear, .hh [about our=
 9   IR:                   [A' right.            [Fine.
10   IE:  =language here [Bill. I never said it.
11→  IR:                 [I'm vi::le because, I'm looking out.
12→       for, (.) late term fetuses who you believe have no rights
13→       at a:ll
```

Again, the IR produces a form of tribuneship that positions him as "looking out" for a particular group in society and does corresponding, negative alignment work for the IE. In lines 11–13, the IR acts as tribune not just for a sectoral interest, but for a sector which cannot, in fact, represent itself: "late-term fetuses." In advocating for the interests of this non-speaking category, the IR also positions the IE in alignment with an opposing group: those responsible for the implied view that late-term fetuses: "have no rights at a:ll."

In all of the above examples it is noticeable that the tribuneship move is made in the context of disagreements. It therefore seems that tribuneship may not simply be a means of adopting a populist stance or speaking for the general public—or particular ideologically delineated sectors of the populace. It is a device whereby those extraneous interests are invoked in the construction of a dispute between IR and IE. In the CPI and API the device can enable a dispute to be prosecuted neutralistically, while in the HPI, the IR's agency and alignment are foregrounded in disputes conducted non-neutralistically.

A HISTORIC SPOTLIGHT INTERVIEW: OBAMA AND GUILT BY THE "ASSOCIATIONS"

I next want to examine in closer detail the complex ways in which tribuneship—understood thus as the tendentious invocation of the public in pursuit of particular agendas—operates in the context of a particularly significant, and controversial, spotlight political interview: Barack Obama's 2008 pre-election interview with Bill O'Reilly on the latter's long-running Fox News show. This interview had a special salience for American and world politics, because Barack Obama would shortly go on to become the first ever African American politician to be elected president of the United States. In a country still deeply affected by its history of race relations, many had doubted that such a momentous event could ever occur. In addition, Obama, standing for the Democratic Party, ran his campaign on one of the most left-wing policy programs that had been seen for decades in the United States. In the early days of the campaign, therefore, there were plenty of reasons other than his ethnic background to doubt that this little-known senator from Chicago would end up being elected president.

During the campaign, the three senators who were competing to replace outgoing president George W. Bush (John McCain, Barack Obama and Hillary Clinton) all gave extended interviews to Fox News' influential nightly show *The O'Reilly Factor*, each of them broadcast in a series of four instalments on consecutive nights. The first in the series was with possibly the favorite to win, Senator Hillary Rodham Clinton toward the end of April 2008, when she was still competing in a very close race with Senator Barack Obama for the Democratic Party presidential nomination. A few weeks later in June 2008, Senator John McCain gave his series of interviews, after his competitors Rudy Giuliani and Mitt Romney dropped out of the Republican nomination race back in February. It was not until September 2008, after he had been confirmed as the Democratic nominee over Clinton, that the third of these interviews was held with Senator Barack Obama.

One of the most potentially explosive aspects of Obama's 2008 election campaign were the reports that emerged concerning his associations with political activists on what was considered to be the far left of American politics. These included his membership, in the past, in the Trinity United Church established by controversial preacher the Reverend Jeremiah Wright. The controversy surrounding Reverend Wright centered upon his interpretations, in his sermons, of the writings of black liberation theologists such as James H. Cone, who in the late 1960s had developed the view that mainstream Christianity in America was complicit in the oppression of black people (Cone, 1970). At the time of the election campaign, certain television news stations were broadcasting undercover footage of the Reverend Wright's sermons in which he appeared to be arguing that the root of America's social problems lay in white power structures and that white people were inherently racist. This story had additional salience given Obama's status as the first ever African American candidate for the presidency of the United States.

A second association picked up by elements of the media, especially cable news and internet sources, was Obama's links with Chicago-based educational activist William (Bill) Ayers, who in his younger days had been a leading member of the Weatherman organization (or Weather Underground). Originally this was an anti–Vietnam War group notorious for its campaign of bombings in American cities in the late 1960s. Ayers later became a professor of education at the University of Illinois at Chicago after turning his attention to community politics and educational reform. Part of the controversy surrounding Ayers stems from the fact that in his writings and interviews he had refused to condemn the Weatherman campaigns and indeed had defended them on the grounds that the bombs had always been targeted at buildings rather than people (Ayers, 2008). At the time of the election campaign, press and broadcast news reported on interviews given by Ayers in which he was quoted as saying that he did not "regret setting bombs" and in fact felt that the Weather Underground did not "do enough" (an interview first published, in a dark twist of fate, on September 11th, 2001, the day of the catastrophic World Trade Center attacks) (Smith, 2001). Although Ayers subsequently maintained that this did not mean he thought that more bombs should have been set (Remnick, 2008), that was the interpretation foregrounded by numerous media outlets reporting on the possible association of Obama with Ayers.

In most liberal democratic societies, but perhaps especially in the USA, any hint of links between a candidate for the head of state and radical individuals and movements such as these would be likely to seriously derail their election campaign. Indeed, the election campaign of Republican candidate John McCain actively sought to foreground these associations in an attempt to destroy Obama's populist image. Yet as we now know, that tactic failed as Obama went on to win the election, and indeed to be re-elected for a second term in 2012, before Donald Trump, in what for many was an even more unexpected victory than Obama's (though for different reasons), brought the presidency back to the Republicans in 2016.

NEGATIVE ATTRIBUTIONS: TRIBUNESHIP, IMPLICATURE AND INSTRUCTION

Let us imagine, for a moment, how the question of Obama's "associations" might have been broached within the modality of the conventional political interview. We might have found a question worded along the following, hypothetical lines:

```
(6) (Invented interview)
1    IR:  Senator Obama, how do you respond to the concerns expressed
2→        by some voters over your supposed associations with figures
3         like the Reverend Wright, Bill Ayers, and the Daily Kos
4→        website whose convention you were reported to have attended
5         recently?
```

Here, we find the standard use of footing shifts and other means of redistributing authorship of claims about controversial matters ("concerns expressed by some voters" or "you were reported to have attended"). The hypothetical CPI interviewer constructs the question without prejudging the answer, so as to allow the matter to be raised in the public interest.

By contrast, the following extract shows the way that the topic was actually broached in the HPI context of the O'Reilly/Obama encounter. The IR and IE sit facing one another in a setting that is not a television studio but has the trappings of a hotel or conference meeting room.

```
(7) O'REILLY FACTOR: Obama Pt 3
1    IR:  I'm sitting here and I'm an American. I'm sitting there in:
2         Bismarck North Dakota, I'm sitting there in, Coral Springs
3         Florida, and I'm seeing Reverend Wright, I'm seeing Father
4         Pfleger, who thinks Louie Farrakhan's a great guy, I'm seeing
5         Bernadette Dohrn and Bill Ayers, Weather Underground radicals
6         who:, ↑don't think they bombed e↓nough. I'm seeing Moveon dot
7         org, who says "General Betray Us," and I'm seeing you go
8         to a Daily Kos convention, and this week Daily Kos came out
9         and said that,.pt Sarah Palin's Down syndrome baby was birthed
10        by her fifteen year old with no proof. They put that on air.
```

11   And I'm going, g<u>ee</u>, that Barack O<u>ba</u>ma, he's got some pretty
12   ↓ba::d ↓friends.

Structurally speaking, though it may not seem so, there are in fact similarities here with the hypothetical example in extract (6). But in terms of the turn's content, the way the issue of the "associations" is put to the interviewee, the differences are quite fundamental.

In one sense, the turn incorporates a footing shift in Goffman's (1981) original sense. The IR begins by taking up the standpoint of a third party, "an American" (line 1), then describes a number of events in the public sphere that the first person American is "seeing" (lines 3–10); then attributes a thought or utterance to that American (line 11): "g<u>ee</u>, that Barack O<u>ba</u>ma, he's got some pretty ↓ba::d ↓friends." In sum, in the Goffmanian sense, this turn sees the interviewer acting as animator for observations and thoughts that some generic American is both principal and author of.

However, in the context of the broadcast political interview, and by comparison with the invented example in extract (6), there is much more going on here than simply a shift in footing. For one thing, although the IR begins with the statement, "I'm sitting here and I'm an A<u>mer</u>ican," the American identity he is seeking to embody, invoke, or perform is indexed in a particular way. The American is described as sitting in "Bismarck North Dakota" or "Coral Springs Florida." This does the work of conveying that the American we are concerned with here is what we might call the *normative American*: a middling kind of decent, family man, not an inner city dweller or someone particularly associated with any controversial political movements, sitting watching the TV in his living room after work, possibly mulling over who he might vote for.

Having established this normative American, the IR lists a number of individuals he is seeing on the TV screen; but rather than simply naming them, he offers instructions as to how both the IE and the audience should understand or orient toward these individuals. Father Pfleger "thinks Louis Farrakhan's a great guy" (Farrakhan being a highly divisive figure in American racial politics); Bernadette (actually Bernardine) Dohrn and Bill Ayers "don't think they bombed enough." The website moveon.org parodies General Petraeus, the head of the military forces in Iraq, as "General Betray Us" while the Daily Kos website implies, "with no proof," that Republican vice presidential candidate Sarah Palin may have put the life of her Down's Syndrome baby at risk by allowing her to be "birthed by her fifteen year old."

In each of these cases, a tacit contrast is being used to do the interactional work of foregrounding negativity. The contrast is between the views expressed by the cited individuals and organizations, and the views held by the imagined normative American. In other words, it is implied that the normative American thinks that Louis Farrakhan is *not* in fact a great guy, and Father Pfleger is wrong to think he is. The normative American thinks that the Weather Underground in fact bombed *too much* (or indeed that they shouldn't have bombed at all), and Dohrn and Ayers are wrong to think they didn't bomb enough. The normative American thinks that General Petraeus is a soldier serving the American national interest, and moveon.org is wrong to say that he is betraying Americans. The normative American thinks that Sarah Palin did *not* in fact allow her fifteen-year-old to birth her Down's Syndrome baby, and the Daily Kos is wrong to say that she did.

Similarly, and much more directly, in the statement "and I'm seeing you go to a Daily Kos convention" (lines 7–8), it is implied that the normative American thinks that going to a Daily Kos convention is not something the prospective president of the United States should be doing, and that Barack Obama is wrong for having done so. As in the previous chapter, we find the interviewer attributing personal responsibility for reprehensible actions to the interviewee through the use of first- and second-person pronouns.

A second aspect of personalization that is key in this particular HPI context is something that is difficult to convey in the form of a transcript on the page: the mounting distaste that is palpable in the IR's voice and facial expression as this list of negative attributions is produced. In such a way, as well as embodying the normative American through the footing shift, "I'm sitting here and I'm an American," the IR here *emotionally* embodies a negative stance toward the things the normative American is witnessing. He thus acts as something more than simply the animator, in Goffman's sense, for this imaginary American's standpoint. Particularly in the emotionally heightened way that he enunciates the final sentence, "An' I'm going, gee, that Barack Obama, he's got some pretty ↓ba::d ↓friends," his voice becoming a raspy whisper in the final two words, the IR establishes a personal identification between the normative American and *himself*.

As we saw previously, news interviewers will often produce statements of some length prior to the production of a question. These statements, even if formulated neutralistically, can be used to negatively pre-position the interviewee, making him or her account for duplicitous acts, failure to see through a promise, or other complainable actions (Pomerantz, 1989). This extended preface similarly does the work of negatively pre-positioning the IE; but it does so less neutralistically by placing him in association with influences defined as negative by the IR himself, in terms of the hypothetically commonsense views of an imagined American citizen and voter.

In the CPI, question prefaces are always followed by a question, and the interviewee typically refrains from responding until the question itself has been asked (Greatbatch, 1988). In the HPI, by contrast, questions may not always follow interviewer statements. Although the HPI does utilize the standard sequential structures of *question-answer-next question* or *question-answer-formulation*, in many cases the question-answer sequence is abandoned in favor of the more argumentative sequence structures of *assertion-counter assertion* or *accusation-response*. Sometimes an interview will begin with a question and answer and then run to completion with no further question-formatted turns being produced by the interviewer.

In the next extract, which follows directly from the conclusion of the question preface in extract (7), we see that the IE in fact begins on a response at a recognizable completion point of the preface; that is, without waiting for a following question (line 13). In other words, he orients to this as the sequential slot in which he should embark on accounting for himself in terms of the negative attributions. However, in this case, it turns out that the IR does tag a question onto the prefacing statement, in overlap with IE's start-up (line 14):

```
(8) O'REILLY FACTOR: Obama Pt 3

11    IR:   And I'm going, gee, that Barack Obama, he's got some
12          pretty ↓ba::d ↓friends.
13→   IE:   All ri[ght, well-
14→   IR:         [Am I wro:ng?=
15    IE:   =You are wrong.
```

The phrase "Am I wrong?" does two types of work here. First, it reformats the turn as a whole into a question; thus, at least superficially, offering some mitigation for the previous negative pre-positioning of the interviewee. More significantly, whether intentionally or not, it provides a question format by means of which the IE can shift from having to *account* for the preceding list of negative connotations, and instead begin by *agreeing* that those connotations are in fact wrong; as indeed he does by restarting his turn in line 15.

At this point, having embarked on a response by agreeing that the IR's characterizations are wrong, normatively within the interview frame the space would be open to the IE to elaborate on why that was the case. As Harris (1991) puts it, a situationally appropriate rule for news interviews is that highly elaborated answers are preferred over simple statements of agreement or disagreement.

But as noted above, a key feature of the HPI is not just the shift between neutralistic and non-neutralistic turn structures, but also between the question-answer frame of the interview and the counter-assertive frame of the argument. We see this quite clearly as the IE begins to expand on his first response:

```
(9) O'REILLY FACTOR: Obama Pt 3

15→   IE:    =You are wrong. Le-lu-lu-Let's, s-start from scratch.
16           .h Number one. (.) I know:: (.) thousands'a people. (.)
17           Right? And so:, understandably, people will pick out,
18           folks who: they think they ca[n  (              )
19→   IR:                                 [I don't know anybody like
20           that. An' I know thousands'a people=I don't know anybody
21           like that.
```

The IE begins by arguing that, among the "thousands" of people that he knows, there may be individuals that certain folk will pick out for politically motivated reasons. The implication here, of course, is that his thousands of other acquaintances are people whom the normative American would find perfectly acceptable.

However, the IR comes in interruptively (line 19) with an immediate counter-position that is based on the premise that it is possible—indeed preferable—to know "thousands" of people without a single one of them being "like that." Moreover, in this counterargument, the IR foregrounds his own agency, and therefore his identification with the counter-position, by nominating himself as such a knower of thousands of people, though he does not know "anybody like that."

The techniques of turn design and sequence construction used in the HPI were here deployed to construct an argument around Barack Obama's political and religious associations. The strategy centered around presenting these associates as negative figures, and as aspects of his political profile that Obama should be required to account for. The IR used aspects of standard interviewing technique, such as the footing shift, in highly non-neutral ways so as to establish himself as the tribune of a hypothetical, tendentiously constructed but nonetheless rhetorically effective public, the "normative American," seeing a range of persons and organizations linked to the IE as "bad." As Obama himself described it, later in the interview, this was a strategy of "classic guilt by association."

154   Chapter Eight

GOING META: WHOSE PEOPLE? WHOSE AGENDA?

I began this chapter by remarking that the question of tribuneship can easily become one of who, in fact, "the people" are, which "people" we are talking about, and who has the power ultimately to delineate which sector of "the people" are being addressed in any given question-answer exchange. In the final example below I examine a remarkable recent interview in which, largely through the actions of the interviewee, the whole question of neutrality versus non-neutrality, agenda-driven questions, and what is in the best interests of "the people" becomes the subject of the interview itself.

It is interesting to note that this interview does not come from a cable news HPI context, but from the mainstream, highly respected and long-running British news and current affairs broadcast, Channel 4 News. It is also worth pointing out that, somewhat bizarrely, the interview is conducted not in a television studio but in a farmyard, the IR putting questions about government policy to the IE, minister Michael Gove, while in the background the lowing of cows can clearly be heard. I am not suggesting that this has anything to do with the nature of the exchange analyzed, but it is contextual information that cannot be derived from the data as presented, since I have decided not to include the sounds of the cattle in the transcript.

The extract begins at a point where the interviewer asks a question about the government's recently announced major investment in new hospitals across the country. Prime minister Boris Johnson has stated that he plans to build forty new hospitals in the next few years; however, the Labor opposition claims that the government's investment plans only include six new hospitals. The IR begins by putting this discrepancy to the IE:

```
(10) CHANNEL 4 NEWS: Gove-Hinds

1      IR:     Forty new hospitals is- is that true or false
2              Minister=Boris Johnson says [forty new hospitals.
3      IE:                                 [Yes it is.
4      IR:     That's [true.
5      IE:            [Yes it is. .hh But I think the
6              critic[al thing-
7      IR:           [You think it's true.
8      IE:     I think the critical thing Ciaran is that, .hh
9              if you want tuh ha:ve e:r er,[ a    p r o p e r    =
10     IR:                                 [But there might only=
```

```
11    IE:    =[conversation
12    IR:    =[be six new hospitals Mr [Gove
13    IE:                               [Er no there'll be forty.
14           .h=If you want to have a proper conversation then
15           we can have a proper conversation. .hh But erm of
16           course what you want to do is to:: .h mount a
17           polemical case=and of course that's=.h=that's
18           perfect[ly legitimate
19    IR:           [This is called scrutiny Mr Gove I'm just
20           asking you simple questions about what is true
21           or not and the voters can make up their minds.
```

As we see, the IE does offer answers to the IR's question, but these answers are produced only as bare affirmations that the claim about forty new hospitals is true (lines 3 and 5; also line 13). For one thing, this type of answer, while it may indeed be a type-conforming answer, in yes/no form, to the polar question put by the interviewer, breaches Harris's (1991: 82) situational appropriacy norm that applies for news interviews. As she puts it, "in the context of a political interview we expect politicians to elaborate, even when asked questions which request a 'yes/no' response." Thus, even in the shape of the type-conforming responses he gives to the IR, there are already clear signs from the IE of unwillingness to cooperate in treating this exchange as "an interview."

That lack of cooperation becomes fully evident from line 14 onwards. At this point the IE "goes meta" with a turn that, rather than being a response to any particular question put by the IR, proposes to instruct the IR about what kind of agenda underpins his chosen questions and about what kind of interactional activity he takes it is in play here. The IE distinguishes between having a "proper conversation," which by implication means some kind of objective or neutralistic exchange (i.e., a conventional interview), and mounting "a polemical case," which is what he suggests the IR is doing.

In response, the IR also abandons for the moment his role of questioner and seeks to defend his line of questioning in journalistic terms, as "scrutiny." At this point (lines 19–21) we find the first of what will become numerous acts of tribuneship in this exchange. By asking "simple questions about what is true or not" the IR presents himself, not as an ideologically driven polemicist, but as the objective scrutineer seeking truth in the interests of the general public, so that "the voters can make up their minds."

156 Chapter Eight

These two contrasting versions of "what is going on" in this particular case are pursued further as the encounter progresses. In the following extract from a minute or so later, we see the same positions being articulated, and this time both the IR *and* the IE, in different ways, seek to act as a tribune with the best interests of the public in mind.

```
(11) CHANNEL 4 NEWS: Gove-Hinds

78    IE:   .h An' objective criteria are important in elections,
79          .h=as are- i:s the expression of opinion. .hh And
80          you want to express a particular opinion, .h and
81          I'm, I'm f:ine with that, .hh but I think it's
82→         only fair that Channel Four viewers recognize,
83          .hh that what you're doing is putting forward,
84          .h a particular point of view, in order
85          to create a, .h particular argument, .hh an'
86→         again that's fine=people will kno:w, .h
87          that you're [arguing,
88→   IR:               [Yihsee people will be very
89→         confused about what you're talking about
90          cuz we're asking fuh simple facts the simple
91          truth [(          )
92    IE:         [No=nuh=no. No no I th[ink people will know-
93    IR:                               [Let's talk about
94          Bre[xit and getting Brexit done  cuz  that's ]=
95    IE:     [I think people will kno::w- I think people]=
96    IR:   =[what you're here to say isn' [it  talk  about ]=
97    IE:   =[will know-                   [I think- I think]=
98    IR:   =[getting Brexit-
99→   IE:   =[I no no I think people will know exactly, what
100         you're doing Ciaran at this point, .h which is
101         mounting, a rigorous left wing case, .h for a
102         particular political point of view=and that
```

```
103         i:s, fine. .hh People know that, they know
104         that's what you and Channel Four news do:,
105         .hhh and then it's only fair, .hh that
106→        people can make a judgement about that.
```

In the arrowed lines here, both IE and IR make claims, from their different standpoints, to be acting in the interests of "people." The IE continues his attack on the "polemical" nature of the IR's questioning, stating that it is important that "people know" what he is up to so that they can "make a judgement" about it. He first of all refers only to "Channel Four viewers" (line 82); but later, in lines 103–104, expands his tribuneship constituency, claiming that "people know" that Channel 4 News regularly engages in mounting "a rigorous left wing case .h for a particular point of view." Meanwhile the IR again abandons his stance as questioner (lines 88-91) in order to establish his own tribuneship of the "people" who will in turn be "confused" by the IE's behavior, since all "we're" doing (that is, Channel 4 News) is "asking fuh simple facts the simple truth."

One thing suggested by this final example is that among certain political circles there is an increasing confidence in taking on the media, and political reporting in particular, for some perceived ideological bias. This tendency includes the promulgation of the concept of "fake news," a phrase particularly popularized in the press conferences of Donald Trump. President Trump famously began his first White House press conference by calling the reporters seated in front of him liars and inventors of news stories, dismissing the BBC as "another beauty" of a fake news organization, and silencing its White House correspondent, Jon Sopel's question with the dismissive phrase, "Sit down. I know who you are."

Of course, it is this kind of treatment, in part, that drives the theory of "post-truth politics" (D'Ancona, 2017; Davies, 2017; Rabin-Havt, 2016): something I return to in more detail in the final chapter. The politician who appears in extracts (10) and (11) above, Michael Gove, is well-known in the UK for his comments in interviews and other statements on the theme that the public have "had enough of experts," thus feeding a favored trope in the post-truth thesis that people in modern democracies are no longer interested in "truth" or "facts" but only in populist emotional appeals. And as we saw in extracts (10) and (11), the journalist himself responded to Mr. Gove's attack on his questioning by asserting that what he was seeking to establish were "simple facts the simple truth."

Whether this represents a strengthening of the case for a post-truth politics overall, or whether such cases are examples of maverick politicians with particular ideological fascinations, who in the future, with the failure of Trump to win a second term in 2021 and the instatement of the more conventional Democrat Joe Biden as US president, will fade into insignificance as a more equilibrious and consensual political order reasserts itself, it is not possible to say. On that, the jury, as they say, is out.

Chapter Nine

The Political Interview in an Opinionated World

Some Concluding Reflections

The main aim of this book has been to show some of the key ways in which, as a form of institutional talk-in-interaction, the broadcast political interview has evolved, and is continuing to evolve, focusing mainly on twenty-first century developments. Examining interviews with politicians in a range of televised formats, the book has argued that the general development in recent years has been toward increasingly conflictual interactional relations in the general discourse of the political interview. By training the sharp analytical lens of conversation analysis on the actuality of live broadcast news in a range of program types and interview frameworks, the book has highlighted the changing roles of journalistic neutralism, adversarialism, tribuneship and advocacy in this "interactional combat zone."

There have been two basic themes. The first is that whereas in the first few decades of its existence, from the mid-twentieth century onwards, the political interview can be seen to develop from more deferential beginnings to more adversarial and probing formats, in more recent decades the adversarial and accountability interview styles—while they still exist in most broadcast outlets—have been joined by still more aggressive, tendentious styles of interviewing: a shift from neutralism toward non-neutralism. The second theme is that "the political interview" itself should not be viewed as a singular phenomenon found only in one type of broadcast news outlet. Rather, we have to recognize the extent to which political interviews take different forms and can be found serving many functions in different types of broadcast outlet.

In this latter point, the book diverges somewhat from many previous studies of the discourse of broadcast news interviews. For example, Clayman and Heritage (2002) hold to what I would describe as a fairly traditional conception of the news interview form as it appears on the long-established, mainstream news channels such as CBS, NBC, BBC or ITV. They make a distinction between what they call "elite" and "quasi" news interviews. The "elite journalistic interview" (2002: 340) is one characterized by the set of "basic ground rules for interview conduct" (2002: 338) that were described in chapters 4 and 5 of this book—the conventional and adversarial interview modalities, as I have termed them. For Clayman and Heritage, this elite form should be distinguished from other "quasi-news interview formats" (2002: 339), which appear in "programs resembling news interviews,"

> involving highly opinionated hosts who are not bound by the norm of neutralism. The news interview now exists alongside, and in competition with, these other formats. Moreover, it exists within a context that is shaped by these formats, in particular the decline in deference and reduction in social distance between journalists and interviewees. (Clayman and Heritage, 2002: 340)

In contrast, I have argued that the "quasi" interview formats themselves, in as much as they are, in fact, interviews with political actors about political ideas, agendas, strategies and policies, should be taken fully into account alongside other, more established forms if we want to reach anything like a complete understanding of the current lie of the land in contemporary broadcast political journalism. We exist, as Chadwick (2014) has said, in a hybrid media environment, and one of the main arguments running through the book has been that the political interview itself, while on the one hand an integral part of this hybrid media system, is also a hybridized phenomenon, taking many shapes and drawing on various conventions of talk-in-interaction to pursue an overall project of holding political actors to account in the interests of "the people"—or in many cases, certain ideologically circumscribed sectors of "the people."

One question that arises here is whether these developments, these evolutionary shifts, are somehow related to other changes in relations between politics, the news media and the public, taking place in the modern democratic world. For if we live in a hybridized media environment, one inescapable and much reported consequence is that we also live in an increasingly opinionated world, in which different media formats support not only the reporting (from whatever standpoint or perspective) on events as they occur in society, but also the promulgation of multiple and competing views *about* those events and the individuals involved in them.

"THEY'RE TRYING TO IGNORE US"

A basic contention of this book is that, while it is diversifying in form and while, in the process, challenges to the traditional neutralistic conception of the interviewer are becoming more apparent, the broadcast political interview remains a key journalistic tool in the overall task of holding politicians to account in modern democracies. It turns out that this is not necessarily a view shared by some media sociologists, and even some journalists and news executives.

For example, in a recent speech, Dorothy Byrne, formerly the head of news and current affairs at UK broadcaster Channel 4, complained that leading politicians in the current environment are increasingly "declining to appear on major news programs to subject themselves to scrutiny." She went on:

> In evil regimes the first thing they do is arrest or kill the journalist . . . What's happened here is that they've not arrested us, they've not killed us, they're trying to ignore us. (Waterson, 2019: 1)

It is of course true that the communications machines of modern political leaders in both the UK and USA make extensive use of the apparently "direct" communication channels of Facebook or Twitter—environments in which their messages can be broadcast in increasingly targeted ways and without being subject to rigorous, independent questioning. Although this was originally seen as a positive political strategy—for instance, in Barack Obama's campaign for the 2008 US presidency, or more recently in the youth-oriented strategies of the Jeremy Corbyn–led Labour Party in the UK—during the presidential incumbency of Donald Trump, in particular, it came to be seen as more of an attempt to hijack the mainstream news agenda. Notoriously, Trump took the Twitter strategy to a new level by regularly communicating his often contentious views on events via his personal account, sometimes in incendiary ways.

These attempts to grasp personal hold of the news agenda occur in, indeed contribute to, an environment where many journalists, like Dorothy Byrne, seem to experience a crisis of legitimacy. In part, this sense of crisis is driven by the very proliferation of news outlets created by the hybrid media system, and the corresponding torrent of unverified and potentially unverifiable news stories that people can experience through their Twitter or Facebook feeds, sometimes drawn under the tendentious banner of "fake news." If a journalist sees their role as reporting on "real" events in the world and impartially holding political actors and other powerful figures to account for their decisions and actions, it is easy to see how the increasing difficulty there might be in distinguishing "fake news" from the rest could lead them to question their role in society.

However, claims that politicians are "trying to ignore" the media's attempts to hold them to account are not really new. Such concerns are grounded in the original nineteenth-century Anglo-American model of journalism as a "high-toned and responsible moral arbiter [engaging] with a reasoned, articulate and mostly stable public invested in public events" (Zelizer, 2019: 142). In this sense, some form or other of legitimation crisis between journalists and politicians can be traced back at least to the Cold War (Zelizer, 2019).

More recently, we can look to the case of the Iraq Wars of 1991, under the presidency of George H. W. Bush, and 2003 under the tenure of his son, George W. Bush. During this time, it transpires that there was a quite explicit attempt, within the camps advising each president, to take on the media and strategically outflank journalists' way of seeing the world. Consider the following, candid account of how government relates to the media given by a White House insider, identified only as a "senior administration official" (but widely thought to be Karl Rove, George W. Bush's chief advisor), in a 2002 piece by Ron Susskind for the magazine *Esquire*:

> The aide said that guys like me were "in what we call the reality-based community," which he defined as people who "believe that solutions emerge from your judicious study of discernible reality." I nodded and murmured something about enlightenment principles and empiricism. He cut me off. "That's not the way the world really works anymore," he continued. "We're an empire now, and when we act, we create our own reality. And while you're studying that reality—judiciously, as you will—we'll act again, creating other new realities, which you can study too, and that's how things will sort out. We're history's actors . . . and you, all of you, will be left to just study what we do." (Cited in Haslett, 2016)

Built into this account is, of course, a dismissal of the idea that politicians should be held to account for their decisions, or their actions. The "reality" they create through their actions is simply there to be observed. This is prescient of the notion of "post-truth" politics, which emerged over a decade later (Rabin-Havt, 2016; D'Ancona, 2017; Evans, 2017). In a "post-truth" society, it is argued, politicians have discovered that they can deal in untruths—or in the phrase of one British politician, be "economical with the truth"—more or less with impunity, or at least without what used to be the ultimate sanction of personal disgrace and resignation from office.

Primarily, the adoption of this position among many modern journalists has been driven by a series of political events that challenged many of the basic assumptions of liberal political thinking. In particular, in the US, the 2016 presidential election of Donald Trump, and in the same year in the UK, the close but decisive vote to leave the European Union ("Brexit"), followed in 2019 by the election as prime minister of the "Vote Leave" campaign's figurehead, Boris Johnson. These events are each interpreted within a wider narrative that highlights a shift toward right-wing populism in world politics; one that the liberal journalistic mindset seems unable to find a way of assimilating. Zelizer (2019: 140) puts it in particularly colorful terms:

> Leaving two of the world's oldest liberal democracies in uncharted waters, the phenomenon of Brexit and Trump highlight how similar the United Kingdom and the United States are to every other location wrestling with nativism, populism, xenophobia, racism, demagoguery and new strains of nationalism. They throw Anglo-American journalism's imaginary into disarray, with elitism, insularity and false confidence rendering it unable to engage meaningfully with current events.

In some accounts, this is linked to a still more fundamental "epistemic crisis" in modern political journalism (Benkler, Faris and Roberts, 2018; Steensen, 2019), that is, a crisis in the grounding of knowledge through which journalism traditionally staked its claims to be reporting the "truth."

> The main drivers of this crisis are discourses of disinformation and the general datafication of society, which combined render dubious the ways in which journalism assesses sources and information in its production of knowledge. Basic journalistic competencies related to information literacy—which constitute a key prerequisite for journalism's ability to establish trust, authenticity and accountability—are out of tune with the challenges of modern information societies. (Steensen, 2019: 185)

What is interesting here is that, after decades of denouncing the tendency toward conspiracy theories as the domain of far right-wing crackpots, many liberal and left-wing writers and journalists now readily cite conspiracy theories of their own about the dark forces out there somewhere undermining reason: "discourses of disinformation" such as foreign powers using the internet to interfere with democracy, or shady "big data" corporations manipulating individuals' personal identities and even their beliefs. Underpinning the whole perspective is the notion that good scientific rationalism has suddenly been supplanted by forms of cultural and ideological relativism. It is almost as if, were it not for these kind of "dark interventions," the victories of Donald Trump and Vote Leave in 2016 would have been different, because "reason" would have prevailed.

This is not to suggest that there is no value in claims about the power of the internet to invade privacy, engage in hidden persuasion, or manipulate data and generate fake news. But it is strange that liberal thinking, at least in some quarters, seems to prefer these explanatory factors over others such as the anger of the neglected working class and underclass in places like the American rust belt or the ex-industrial "migrant dumping" towns of the English north as the key factor behind people's decisions to vote for Trump or Brexit. Such people are not persuaded by the kinds of bourgeois metropolitan "Project Fear" launched by Trump's opponents or the Remain campaign in the Brexit referendum; in fact, they are likely to feel even more marginalized, and thus angry, as a result.

In the end, post-truth thinking and the notion of epistemic crisis are as much as anything about a particular journalistic conception of how the world should be. As Collins (2019: 15) puts it, "what concerns around post-truth suggest is not a new and distinct threat to rational political discourse, but an expression of liberal journalism's loss of faith in its own validity."

In many ways, it is this loss of faith that leads to the notion that important forms of political discourse, such as the news interview, are becoming less important. But is it really the case that politicians increasingly live in a world of their own making, immune from accountability? It is not difficult to come up with examples that suggest it is at least a selective version of reality. For example, in early 2021, former French President Nicolas Sarkozy was sentenced to jail for three years, convicted of attempting to bribe a judge. Donald Trump was, unprecedentedly, impeached twice during his presidency, though both times the motion failed to pass in the Senate. Nevertheless, despite his own conspiratorial claims about fraud, corruption and external influence in the 2021 election, he lost his bid to serve a second term in the White House in favor of Democrat Joe Biden. Some politicians have always "got away with it." Others continue to be held to account by the legal, political, and indeed journalistic institutions that underpin democracy.

In sum, it is not difficult to see that there is a good degree of hyperbole about claims that, as Waterson (2019) puts it, "The political interview is not dead—but it is on life support." Not only has it always been comparatively rare for incumbent heads of state to subject themselves to live one-to-one television interviews, but a simple YouTube search will show that over the last few years Johnson, Trump, Obama and other recent leaders *have* in fact appeared numerous times in set-piece televised interviews, in a variety of both mainstream and hybrid news outlets.

Indeed, in the UK, during the 2019 general election campaign, the televised political interview itself took center stage at one point. A key issue emerged around how many, and crucially, *which* television interviewers each of the party leaders agreed to face in the usual pre-election round of spotlight interviews. Specifically, Jeremy Corbyn (then Labour Party leader) having faced a very tough time at the hands of veteran interviewer Andrew Neil on the BBC, the question was raised as to whether Boris Johnson (Conservative leader) would appear on the same show. Johnson seemed unsure, and Neil went so far as to broadcast a specially recorded, directly addressed invitation to Johnson to appear on his program: a rare if not unprecedented move which might be open to interpretation as a proposition to "man up." In the end, Johnson did decline to be interviewed by Neil; although it is worth pointing out that not long afterward, he agreed to appear in what became a highly combative, thirty-minute interview with another high-profile BBC journalist, Andrew Marr.

It may well be the case at present that certain politicians seem increasingly confident in taking on the news media's agendas. We saw quite clear examples of this in the final section of chapter 8. But reports of the news interview's imminent demise must be taken with a pinch of salt. As Clayman and Heritage (2002: 343) argue, the significance of the interview as a format for challenging political evasiveness may simply vary according to the political climate of the day:

> It is more likely that politicians can get away with uninformative answers and set-piece statements during periods of political consensus, or when a particular party or ideological position dominates the political agenda. However, during times of intense debate or discussion, or when a political party or administration is in disarray, the balance of opportunity tends to favor the interviewer, and a medium that previously seemed played out renews itself as an instrument of journalistic inquiry.

In his account of the growth of the accountability interview within broadcast news, Montgomery (2007: 216) also suggests that moves away from the conventions of neutralism, not just in so-called "quasi-news interview formats," but in the discourse of mainstream news interviewing too, may be associated with the erosion of consensus around moral values in many areas of social and political life, with the result that "quite simply, more positions are contestable, fewer taken for granted." Consequently, challenges to neutralism may come from "an evolution in how the role of the interviewer is understood."

> Moral positions may seem at one moment incommensurable but in an incommensurable moral world the accountability interviewer increasingly finds it difficult to insulate him or herself from every position. Instead they assume the role not just of "tribune of the people" simply pursuing the truth on behalf of the audience through question and answer, but also on occasion the role of "arbiter of truth." (Montgomery, 2007: 216)

In the discourses of post-truth and epistemic crisis, the idea of a morally incommensurable world has a different effect on political journalism. Amid claims that rationalism has been supplanted by relativism, public trust in the authenticity of expertise has been eroded in favor of the emotional and instinctual discourses of populism, and "facts" have become replaced by "perspectives," journalists are entreated to repair their "outmoded" practices. The solutions put forward, however, often seem vague, generic, or even rhetorical:

> The list of corrections is enormous: listening more actively, treating class and race as more than disruptions, developing social media accountability, bonding together, seeking out alternative political sources, developing new beats, improving local news, newsroom diversity, media literacy and fact-checking . . . getting rid of condescension or understanding that anger at elites includes them. (Zelizer, 2019: 151–2)

In this book, by contrast, I have not sought to provide solutions or recommendations for how political interviews should be conducted in an increasingly opinionated world and an increasingly hybridized media environment. Instead, I have offered a more empirical approach, beginning from the notion that what we need to do is to *analyze* the changing dimensions of political interviews, the better to understand how news—particularly broadcast news—is shaped by its interactional structures into the broadcast talk that its audiences encounter. It is with this "analytic imperative" that I will conclude the book.

THE ANALYTIC IMPERATIVE

For many sociologists, the relationship between journalism and "facts," "truth" or "reality" has never been as straightforward as the liberal notion of post-truth politics would suggest. Without going so far as adopting wholesale cultural relativism, it is not difficult to appreciate that no single representation of reality can ever hope to account for every possible perspective or interpretation of events. The news therefore can only ever comprise a constructed, decision-based, and thus inevitably partial, representation of "facts" or "truth." As a series of influential sociological, ethnographic and linguistic studies of news production have shown, the task of social science is not to evaluate the relative truth value of news but to understand the processes by which events are processed through the news-gathering procedures of journalists and news organizations to produce the construction of reality that makes up "the news" as it appears in the public sphere (Gans, 1979; Schlesinger, 1978; Tuchman, 1978; Fowler, 1991).

It is, of course, perfectly legitimate for sociologists to have it as their business to adopt critical standpoints on whether or not we live in a "post-truth" society, and indeed, whether or not that means that televised political journalism has any real impact, or any real future. Similarly, there are sociolinguistic perspectives that would wish to look into the power relations, the political economy, or the class, race or gendered underpinnings of these shifts in relations between media and politics.

But the approach I have taken in this book has been different. It has been to observe and to analyze the forms and formats of the political interview as they can be found at this point in history, beamed out by our televised news outlets. As I began by outlining in chapter 2, conversation analysis is not a methodology that sanctions theorizing about what is right or wrong about a given, observable state of affairs, or speculating as to the relative truth value of claims made in any given exchange of talk-in-interaction. Its focus is on the forms and structures of talk-in-interaction as phenomena in their own right, as practiced by humans in, and as a constitutive part of, whichever specifiable social context an analyst might choose to investigate.

From a CA standpoint, one of the basic imperatives is to attempt to see the familiar world in which we live, along with those we are studying, as unfamiliar; just as an anthropologist might encounter, and try to make sense of, the language, rituals and practices of a newly discovered culture. That includes the sometimes difficult task of remaining analytically indifferent about the social activities that we can see going on around us, and being open to seeing, and analyzing, the ways in which those activities are achieved by the participants involved in them, primarily through their turn-by-turn organization of talk.

I used this as a starting point to develop an analytical narrative about the development of news interview formats. The basic norms of neutralism that structure the "elite" news interview, even in its more adversarial guises, were shown to represent an interactional baseline for interviewer/interviewee conduct that is found in its purest sense in the turn-taking practices of the conventional political interview. These interactional conventions were then shown to develop, to be modified or modulated, as the mode of behavior becomes more challenging, more aggressive, more assertoric, particularly on the part of IRs; and more slippery and evasive—or alternatively, epistemically assertive—on the part of IEs.

Thus, unlike Clayman and Heritage (2002), but in a way closer to Montgomery's (2007) approach, I have distinguished *between* the conventional and the adversarial political interview types. By extension, Montgomery's "accountability" interview, for me, is best seen as a particularly extreme version of the adversarial political interview, or, better, as a form that is intermediate between the harder end of the adversarial interview and the softer end of what I have called the hybrid political interview.

From a CA perspective, moves toward non-neutralism in non-mainstream news programs are as interesting as moves toward non-neutralism in mainstream programs, and vice versa. We have seen that, currently, the tendency toward blending interview with argument is more pronounced in non-mainstream outlets. But at the same time, we have seen that there is evidence that a similar tendency is increasingly apparent in some mainstream interview practices. Future research needs to trace this new evolutionary direction in further detail.

In the end, then, what we as social scientists are charged with, instead of arguing over whose version of reality is more "truthy," whose "facts" are more incontestable, or whose studies on which those facts are based is more methodologically reliable, is the imperative to *analyze* the disputes, the agenda contests, the attempts to hold politicians to account and the attempts to evade that accountability, that we can find out there in the world, and to reach at least some understanding of how the structures of language and interaction are marshalled, by human agents, in pursuit of those activities.

Appendix
Glossary of Transcription Symbols

Conversation analysis uses as its data recordings of actual interactions drawn from the naturally-occurring settings in which humans talk to one another. To facilitate detailed analysis based on repeated listenings, the tapes are transcribed using a system, the main aim of which is to provide a sense, in written form, of how a stretch of talk "sounds" on the tape. The aim is not to produce a phonetic transcript, but an interactional one: one that focuses on how the talk is interactionally organized among the participants in real time. For that reason, the main things to look out for when reading the transcripts presented in these chapters are symbols indicating stress or emphasis, pauses, loudness or quietness, and overlapping or interruptive talk. The full set of symbols used in the book are listed below; they are the standard conventions within the field of conversation analysis, and were developed by the late Dr. Gail Jefferson, one of the founding figures of that field.

Symbol Explanation

(0.5)	Numbers in brackets indicate a gap timed in tenths of a second.
(.)	A dot enclosed in brackets indicates a "micropause" of less than one tenth of a second.
=	Equal signs are used to indicate 'latching' or absolutely no discernible gap between utterances; or to show the continuation of a speaker's utterance across intervening lines of transcript.
[ ]	Square brackets indicate the points where overlapping talk starts (left bracket) and ends (right bracket). Although the start of an overlap is always marked, the end is only sometimes marked.
[[	Double left square brackets indicate turns that start simultaneously.

( )	Empty parentheses indicate the presence of an unclear utterance or other sound on the tape.
(( ))	Double parentheses are used to describe a non-verbal activity: for example ((banging sound)). They are also used to enclose the transcriber's comments on contextual or other relevant features.
.hhh	h's preceded by a dot are used to represent audible inward breathing. The more h's, the longer the breath.
hhhh	h's with no preceding dot are used in the same way to represent outward breathing.
huh-huh heh-hah hih-hee	Laughter is transcribed using "laugh tokens" which, as far as the transcriber is able, represent the individual sounds that speakers make while laughing.
sou:::nd	Colons indicate the stretching of a sound or a word. The more colons the greater the extent of the stretching.
sou-	A dash indicates a word suddenly cut off during an utterance.
. , ?	Punctuation marks are not used grammatically, but to indicate prosodic aspects of the talk.
.	A full stop or period indicates a falling tone, not necessarily the end of a sentence.
,	Commas indicate fall-rise or rise-fall (a "continuing" tone).
?	Question marks indicate a marked rising tone, not necessarily a question.
↑↓	Upward and downward arrows are used to show a marked rise or fall in pitch across a phrase.
a̲:	Underlining of a letter before a colon indicates a small drop in pitch during a word.
a:̲	Underlining of a colon after a letter indicates a small rise in pitch at that point in the word.
Underline	Other underlining indicates speaker emphasis. Words may be underlined either in part or in full, depending on the enunciation.
CAPITALS	Capitals mark a section of speech markedly louder than that surrounding it.
→	Arrows in the left margin point to specific parts of the transcript discussed in the text.
° °	Degree signs are used to indicate that the talk between them is noticeably quieter than surrounding talk.

< >	Outward chevrons are used to indicate that the talk between them is noticeably slower than surrounding talk.
> <	Inner chevrons are used to indicate that the talk between them is noticeably quicker than surrounding talk.

References

Arminen, Ilkka. 2005. *Institutional Interaction*. London: Ashgate.
Atkinson, J. Maxwell, and Paul Drew. 1979. *Order in Court: The Organization of Verbal Interaction in Judicial Settings*. London: Macmillan.
Atkinson, J. Maxwell, and John Heritage, eds. 1984. *Structures of Social Action: Studies in Conversation Analysis*. Cambridge: Cambridge University Press.
Atkinson, Paul, and David Silverman. 1997. Kundera's immortality: The interview society and the invention of the self. *Qualitative Inquiry*, 3: 304-325.
Austin, J.L. 1962. *How to Do Things with Words*. Oxford: Clarendon Press.
Ayers, William. 2008. The real Bill Ayers. *The New York Times*, December 6.
Bateson, Gregory. 1956. The message "This is play." In *Group Processes: Transactions of the Second Conference*, edited by Bertram Schaffner, 145-242. New York, NY: Josiah Macy Jr. Foundation.
Bateson, Gregory, and Margaret Mead. 1942. *Balinese Character: A Photographic Analysis*. New York, NY: New York Academy of Sciences.
Baym, Geoffrey. 2013. Transformations in hybrid TV talk: Extended interviews on *The Daily Show (.com)*. In, *Media Talk and Political Elections in Europe and America*, edited by Mats Ekström and Andrew Tolson, 63–86. London: Palgrave Macmillan.
Bell, Allan. 1991. *The Language of News Media*. Oxford: Blackwell.
Benkler, Yochai, Robert Faris, and Hal Roberts. 2018. *Network Propaganda: Manipulation, Disinformation and Radicalization in American Politics*. New York, NY: Oxford University Press.
Berger, Peter, and Thomas Luckmann. 1966. *The Social Construction of Reality: A Treatise in the Sociology of Knowledge*. London: Penguin Books.
Birdwhistell, Ray. 1952. *Introduction to Kinesics: An Annotation System for the Analysis of Body Motion and Gesture*. Washington DC: Foreign Services Institute, US Department of State.
Blumer, Herbert. 1969. *Symbolic Interactionism*. Englewood-Cliffs, NJ: Prentice-Hall.

Boden, Deirdre, and Don Zimmerman, eds. 1991. *Talk and Social Structure*. Cambridge: Polity Press.

Bolden, Galina. 2006. Little words that matter: Discourse markers "so" and "oh" and the doing of other-attentiveness in social interaction. *Journal of Communication*, 56: 661–688.

Bolden, Galina. 2008. "So what's up?": Using the discourse marker 'so' to launch conversational business. *Research on Language and Social Interaction*, 41: 302–327.

Bolden, Galina. 2009. Implementing incipient actions: The discourse marker "so" in English conversation. *Journal of Pragmatics*, 41: 974–98.

Bolden, Galina. 2018. *Nu*-prefaced responses in Russian conversation. In *Between Turn and Sequence: Turn-Initial Particles Across Languages*, edited by John Heritage and Marja-Leena Sorjonen, 5–58. Amsterdam: John Benjamins.

Brants, Kees, and Peter Neijens. 1998. The infotainment of politics. *Political Communication*, 15: 149–164.

Brooker, Charlie. 2011. The Ed Miliband loop and the media reality deficit. *The Guardian*, 3 July.

Bull, Peter. 2008. Slipperiness, evasion and ambiguity. *Journal of Language and Social Psychology*, 27: 333–344.

Bull, Peter, Ralph Negrine, and Katie Hawn. 2014. Telling it like it is or just telling a good story?: Editing techniques in news coverage of the British parliamentary expenses scandal. *Language and Dialogue*, 4: 213–233.

Button, Graham, and Neil Casey. 1985. Topic nomination and topic pursuit. *Human Studies*, 8: 3–55.

Carbaugh, Donal. 1988. *Talking American: Cultural Discourses on Donahue*. Norwood, NJ: Ablex.

Chadwick, Andrew. 2011. The political information cycle in a hybrid news system: The British prime minister and the Bullygate affair. *International Journal of Press/Politics*, 16: 3–29.

Chadwick, Andrew. 2014. *The Hybrid Media System*. Oxford: Oxford University Press.

Chomsky, Noam. 1965. *Aspects of the Theory of Syntax*. The Hague: Mouton.

Clark, Herbert H. 1992. *Arenas of Language Use*. Chicago, IL: University of Chicago Press.

Clayman, Steven E. 1988. Displaying neutrality in television news interviews. *Social Problems*, 35: 474–492.

Clayman, Steven E. 1989. The production of punctuality: Social interaction, temporal organization, and social structure. *American Journal of Sociology*, 95: 659-691.

Clayman, Steven E. 1990. From talk to text: Newspaper accounts of reporter-source interactions. *Media, Culture and Society*, 12: 79–104.

Clayman, Steven E. 1992. Footing in the achievement of neutrality: The case of news interview discourse. In *Talk At Work: Interaction in Institutional Settings*, edited by Paul Drew and John Heritage, 163–198. Cambridge: Cambridge University Press.

Clayman, Steven E. 1995. Defining moments, presidential debates, and the dynamics of quotability. *Journal of Communication*, 45: 118–146.

Clayman, Steven, E. 2002. Tribune of the people: Maintaining the legitimacy of aggressive journalism. *Media, Culture and Society*, 24: 197–216.

Clayman, Steven E. 2010. Address terms in the service of other actions. *Discourse and Communication* 4: 161–183.

Clayman, Steven, and John Heritage. 2002. *The News Interview*. Cambridge: Cambridge University Press.

Clayman, Steven E., and Laura Loeb. 2018. Polar questions, response preference, and the tasks of political positioning in journalism. *Research on Language and Social Interaction*, 51: 127–144.

Clayman, Steven E., and Jack Whalen. 1989. When the medium becomes the message: The case of the Rather-Bush encounter. *Research on Language and Social Interaction*, 22: 241–272.

Coleman, Stephen. 2010. *Leaders in the Living Room–the Prime Ministerial Debates of 2010: Evidence, Evaluation and Some Recommendations*. Oxford: Reuters Institute for the Study of Journalism.

Collins, Jeremy. 2019. "The facts don't work": The EU Referendum campaign and the journalistic construction of "post-truth politics." *Discourse, Context and Media*, 27: 15-21.

Cone, James H. 1970. *A Black Theology of Liberation*. Philadelphia, PA: Lippencott.

Conlan, Tara. 2015. Has Jeremy Corbyn changed the art of political interviewing? *The Guardian*, 4 October.

Corner, John. 1991. The interview as social encounter. In *Broadcast Talk*, edited by Paddy Scannell, 31–47. London: Sage.

Corner, John, Kay Richardson, and Katy Parry. 2013. Comedy, the civic subject, and generic mediation. *Television and New Media*, 14: 31–45.

Coulter, Jeff. 1990. Elementary properties of argument sequences. In *Interaction Competence*, edited by George Psathas, 181–204. Washington DC: University Press of America.

Coulthard, Malcolm. 1977. *An Introduction to Discourse Analysis*. London: Longman.

D'Ancona, Matthew. 2017. *Post-Truth: The New War on Truth*. London: Ebury.

Davidson, Judy. 1984. Subsequent versions of invitations, offers, requests, and proposals dealing with potential or actual rejection. In *Structures of Social Action: Studies in Conversation Analysis*, edited by J. Maxwell Atkinson and John Heritage, 102–128. Cambridge: Cambridge University Press.

Davis, Evan. 2017. *Post-Truth: Why We Have Reached Peak Bullshit*. London: Little, Brown.

Deppermann, Arnulf. 2013. Turn-design at turn-beginnings: Multimodal resources to deal with tasks of turn-construction in German. *Journal of Pragmatics*, 46: 91–121.

Drew, Paul. 1992. Contested evidence in courtroom cross-examination: The case of a trial for rape. In *Talk At Work: Interaction in Institutional Settings*, edited by Paul Drew and John Heritage, 470–520. Cambridge: Cambridge University Press.

Drew, Paul, and John Heritage, eds. 1992. *Talk at Work: Interaction in Institutional Settings*. Cambridge: Cambridge University Press.
Drew, Paul, and John Heritage, eds. 2007. *Conversation Analysis (4 Vols)*. London: Sage.
Ekström, Mats. 2001. Politicians interviewed on television news. *Discourse and Society*, 12: 563–584.
Ekström, Mats. 2011. Hybridity as a resource and challenge in a talk show political interview. In *Talking Politics in Broadcast News*, edited by Mats Ekström and Marianna Patrona, 135–156. Amsterdam: John Benjamins Publishing Company.
Ekström, Mats, and Richard Fitzgerald. 2014. Groundhog day: Extended repetitions in political news interviews. *Journalism Studies*, 15: 82–97.
Ekström, Mats and Bengt Johanssen. 2008. Talk scandals. *Media, Culture and Society*, 30: 61–79.
Ekström, Mats, Asa Kroon and Mats Nylund, eds. 2006. *News from the Interview Society*. Gothenburg: Nordicom.
Ekström, Mats, and Marianna Patrona, eds. 2011. *Talking Politics in Broadcast News*. Amsterdam: John Benjamins.
Ekström, Mats, and Andrew Tolson, eds. 2013. *Media Talk and Political Elections in Europe and the USA*. London: Palgrave Macmillan.
Ekström, Mats, and Andrew Tolson. 2017. Political interviews: Pushing the boundaries of 'neutralism'. In *The Mediated Politics of Europe: A Comparative Study of Discourse*, edited by Mats Ekström and Julie Firmstone, 123–149. London: Palgrave MacMillan.
Eriksson, Göran. 2011. Adversarial moments: A study of short-form interviews in the news. *Journalism*, 12: 51–69.
Eriksson, Göran, and Johan Östman. 2013. Cooperative or adversarial? Journalists' enactment of the watchdog function in political news production. *International Journal of Press/Politics*, 18: 304–324.
Emmertsen, Sophie. 2007. Interviewers' challenging questions in British debate interviews. *Journal of Pragmatics*, 39: 570–591.
Fairclough, Norman. 1995. *Media Discourse*. London: Edward Arnold.
Fairclough, Norman. 2000. *New Labour, New Language*. London: Routledge.
Fowler, Roger. 1991. *Language in the News*. London: Routledge.
Frankel, Richard. 1984. From sentence to sequence: Understanding the medical encounter through microinteractional analysis. *Discourse Processes*, 7: 135–170.
Gans, Herbert. 1979. *Deciding What's News: A Study of CBS Evening News, NBC Nightly News, Newsweek and Time*. New York, NY: Vintage Press.
Garcia, Angela. 1991. Dispute resolution without disputing: How the interactional organization of mediation hearings minimizes argument. *American Sociological Review*, 56: 818–35.
Garfinkel, Harold. 1967. *Studies in Ethnomethodology*. Englewood Cliffs, NJ: Prentice Hall.
Garfinkel, Harold, and Harvey Sacks. 1970. On formal structures of practical actions. In *Theoretical Sociology*, edited by John C. McKinney and Edward A. Tiryakian, 338-366. New York, NY: Appleton-Century-Crofts.

Garton, Greg, Martin Montgomery, and Andrew Tolson. 1991. Ideology, scripts and metaphors in the public sphere of a general election. In *Broadcast Talk*, edited by Paddy Scannell, 100–118. London: Sage.

Golding, Peter, and Philip Elliott. 1979. *Making the News*. London: Longman.

Goffman, Erving. 1956. *The Presentation of Self in Everyday Life*. New York, NY: Random House.

Goffman, Erving. 1981. *Forms of Talk*. Oxford: Blackwell.

Goodwin, M.H. 1990. *He-Said-She-Said: Talk as Social Organization among Black Children*. Bloomington, IN: Indiana University Press.

Greatbatch, David. 1986. Aspects of topical organisation in news interviews: The use of agenda-shifting procedures by interviewees. *Media, Culture and Society*, 8: 441–455.

Greatbatch, David. 1988. A turn-taking system for British news interviews. *Language in Society*, 17: 401–430.

Greatbatch, David. 1992. On the management of disagreement between news interviewees. In *Talk At Work: Interaction in Institutional Settings*, edited by Paul Drew and John Heritage, 268–301. Cambridge: Cambridge University Press.

Green, Damon. 2011. "To a TV reporter . . ." www.twitlonger.com/show/bfnesm, 1/7/2011.

Harris, Sandra. 1991. Evasive action: How politicians respond to questions in political interviews. In *Broadcast Talk*, edited by Paddy Scannell, 76–99. London: Sage.

Haslett, Adam. 2016. "How the Bush dynasty's tactics birthed the President Trump nightmare." *The Guardian*, Friday 19 February.

Hayashi, Makoto. 2009. Marking a "noticing of departure" in talk: *Eh*-prefaced turns in Japanese conversation. *Journal of Pragmatics*, 41: 2100–2129.

Heaney, Seamus. 1999. *Beowulf: A New Translation*. London: Faber and Faber.

Heath, Christian. 1992. The delivery and reception of diagnosis in the general practice consultation. In *Talk At Work: Interaction in Institutional Settings*, edited by Paul Drew and John Heritage, 235–267. Cambridge: Cambridge University Press.

Heritage, John. 1984. A change-of-state token and aspects of its sequential placement. In *Structures of Social Action: Studies in Conversation Analysis*, edited by J. Maxwell Atkinson and John Heritage, 299–345. Cambridge: Cambridge University Press.

Heritage, John. 1985. Analyzing news interviews: Aspects of the production of talk for an overhearing audience. In *Handbook of Discourse Analysis, Volume 3: Discourse and Dialogue*, edited by Teun A. van Dijk, 95–119. London: Academic Press..

Heritage, John. 2013. Turn-initial position and some of its occupants. *Journal of Pragmatics*, 57: 331–337.

Heritage, John, Steven E. Clayman, and Don Zimmerman. 1980. Discourse and message analysis: The micro-structure of mass media messages. In *Advancing Communication Science: Merging Mass and Interpersonal Processes*, edited by Robert P. Hawkins, John M. Wiemann and Suzanne Pingree, 77–109. London: Sage.

Heritage, John, and David Greatbatch. 1991. On the institutional character of institutional talk: The case of news interviews. In *Talk and Social Structure*, edited by Deirdre Boden and Don Zimmerman, 93–137. Cambridge: Polity.

Heritage, John, and Marja-Leena Sorjonen. 1994. Constituting and maintaining activities across sequences: *And*-prefacing as a feature of question design. *Language in Society*, 23: 1–29.

Heritage, John, and Marja-Leena Sorjonen, eds. 2018. *Between Turn and Sequence: Turn-Initial Particles Across Languages*. Amsterdam: John Benjamins.

Hutchby, Ian. 1992. Confrontation talk: Aspects of "interruption" in argument sequences on talk radio. *Text*, 12: 343–371.

Hutchby, Ian. 1996. *Confrontation Talk: Arguments, Asymmetries and Power on Talk Radio*. Mahwah, NJ: Lawrence Erlbaum Associates.

Hutchby, Ian. 2001a. Witnessing: The use of first-hand knowledge in legitimating lay opinions on talk radio. *Discourse Studies*, 3: 481–497.

Hutchby, Ian. 2001b. *Oh*, irony and sequential ambiguity in arguments. *Discourse and Society*, 12: 147–165.

Hutchby, Ian. 2006. *Media Talk: Conversation Analysis and the Study of Broadcasting*. Maidenhead: Open University Press.

Hutchby, Ian. 2008. Participants' orientations to interruptions, rudeness and other impolite acts in talk-in-interaction. *Journal of Politeness Research*, 4: 221–241.

Hutchby, Ian. 2011a. Non-neutrality and argument in the Hybrid Political Interview. *Discourse Studies*, 13: 349–366.

Hutchby, Ian. 2011b. Doing non-neutral: Belligerent interaction in the Hybrid Political Interview. In *Talking Politics in the Broadcast Media*, edited by Mats Ekström and Marianna Patrona, 115–134. Amsterdam: John Benjamins.

Hutchby, Ian, and Robin Wooffitt. 2008. *Conversation Analysis (2nd Edition)*. Cambridge: Polity.

Hutchby, Ian. 2013. Obama in the No Spin Zone. In *Media Talk and Political Elections in Europe and the USA*, edited by Mats Ekström and Andrew Tolson, 41–62. London: Palgrave Macmillan.

James, Oliver. 2013. So, here's a carefully packaged sentence that shows me in my best light. *The Guardian*, Friday 26 July.

Jefferson, Gail. 1986. Notes on latency in overlap onset. *Human Studies*, 9: 153–183.

Jefferson, Gail. 2004. Glossary of transcript symbols with an introduction. In *Conversation Analysis: Studies from the First Generation*, edited by Gene Lerner, 13–34. Amsterdam: John Benjamins.

Jefferson, Gail. 2018. The abominable "ne?": An exploration of post-response pursuit of response. In *Repairing the Broken Surface of Talk*, edited by Paul Drew and Jörg Bergmann, 215–296. Oxford: Oxford University Press.

Kantara, Argyro. 2012. Adversarial challenges and responses in Greek political interviews. *Critical Approaches to Discourse Analysis Across Disciplines*, 5: 171–189.

Kantara, Argyro. 2017. Hearing non-neutral: Listening practices and the construction of societal consensus in hybrid election campaign interviews. *Journalism*, 18: 119–137.

Kantara, Argyro. 2018. Hybridity and antagonism in broadcast election campaign interviews. In *Doing Politics: Discursivity, Perfomativity and Mediation in Political Discourse*, edited by Michael Kranert and Geraldine Horan, 259-280. Amsterdam: John Benjamins.

Keevallik, Leelo. 2012. Compromising progressivity: *No*-prefacing in Estonian. *Pragmatics*, 22: 119–146.

Kendon, Adam. 1990. *Conducting Interaction*. Cambridge: Cambridge University Press.

Kroon Lundell, Asa, and Mats Ekström. 2010. Interview bites in television news production and presentation. *Journalism Practice*, 4: 476–491.

Lauerbach, Gerda. 2004. Political interviews as a hybrid genre. *Text* 24: 353–397.

Lauerbach, Gerda. 2010. Manoeuvring between the political, the personal, and the private: Talk, image and rhythm in TV dialogue. *Discourse and Communication*, 4: 125–160.

Lerner, Gene, ed.. 2004. *Conversation Analysis: Studies from the First Generation*. Amsterdam: John Benjamins.

Levinson, Steven. 1983. *Pragmatics*. Cambridge: Cambridge University Press.

Lewis, Michael. 1999. *The New New Thing: A Silicon Valley Story*. London: Hodder and Stoughton.

Loeb, Laura. 2017. Politicians on celebrity talk shows. *Discourse, Context and Media*, 20: 146–156.

Luginbühl, Martin. 2007. Conversational violence in political TV debates: Forms and functions. *Journal of Pragmatics*, 39: 1371–1387.

Lynch, Micheal, and David Bogen. 1996. *The Spectacle of History: Speech, Text and Memory at the Iran-Contra Hearings*. London: Duke University Press.

Mast, Jelle, Roel Coesemans, and Martina Temmerman, eds. 2017. Special Issue: Hybridity and the News. *Journalism: Theory, Practice and Criticism*, 18: 3–137.

Matheson, Donald. 2005. *Media Discourses: Analyzing Media Texts*. Maidenhead: Open University Press.

Maynard, Douglas W. 1985. How children start arguments. *Language in Society*, 14: 1–29.

Maynard, Douglas, and John Heritage, eds. 2004. *Interaction and Medical Practice*. Cambridge: Cambridge University Press.

McHoul, Alec. 1978. The organisation of turns at formal talk in the classroom. *Language in Society*, 19: 183–213.

Meehan, Eileen R. 2005. *Why TV Is Not Our Fault: Television Programming, Viewers and Who's Really in Control*. Lanham, MD: Rowman & Littlefield.

Montgomery, Martin. 2007. *The Discourse of Broadcast News*. London: Routledge.

Montgomery, Martin. 2010. Rituals of personal experience in television news interviews. *Discourse and Communication*, 4: 185–212.

Montgomery, Martin. 2011. The accountability interview, politics and change in UK public service broadcasting. In *Talking Politics in the Broadcast Media*, edited by Mats Ekström and Mariana Patrona, 33–55. Amsterdam: John Benjamins.

Mullaney, Louise. 2011. *Discursive Approaches to Politeness*. Amsterdam: Mouton de Gruyter.

Nofsinger, Robert. 1989. "Let's talk about the record": Contending over topic redirection in the Rather/Bush interview. *Research on Language and Social Interaction*, 22: 273-292.

Nunberg, Geoff. 2015. So, what's the big deal with starting a sentence with "so"? www.npr.org/2015/09/03/432732859/ (Accessed 1 Nov 2020)

Otto, Lukas, Isabella Glogger, and and Mark Boukes. 2016. The softening of journalistic political communication: A comprehensive framework model of sensationalism, soft news, infotainment, and tabloidization. *Communication Theory*, 27: 136-155.

Patrona, Marianna. 2011. Neutralism revisited: When journalists set new rules in political news discourse. In *Talking Politics in Broadcast Media*, edited by Mats Ekström and Marianna Patrona, 157–176. Amsterdam: John Benjamins.

Pomerantz, Anita. 1984. Agreeing and disagreeing with assessments: Some features of preferred/dispreferred turn-shapes. In *Structures of Social Action: Studies in Conversation Analysis*, edited by J. Maxwell Atkinson and John Heritage, 79–112. Cambridge: Cambridge University Press.

Pomerantz, Anita. 1986. Extreme case formulations. *Human Studies*, 9: 219–30.

Pomerantz, Anita. 1989. Constructing skepticism: Four devices used to engender the audience's skepticism. *Research on Language and Social Interaction*, 22: 293–314.

Porter, Andrew, and Rosa Prince. 2010. General Election 2010: Gordon Brown's Gillian Duffy "bigot" gaffe may cost Labour. *Daily Telegraph*, 28 April.

Rabin-Havt, Ari. 2016. *Lies, Incorporated: The World of Post-Truth Politics*. New York, NY: Anchor Books.

Remnick, David. 2008. Mr Ayers' neighborhood. *The New Yorker*, November 4.

Rendle-Short, Johanna. 2007. Neutralism and adversarial challenges in the political news interview. *Discourse and Communication*, 1: 387–406.

Robinson, Duncan. 2011. Ed Miliband tongue-tied on strikes. *New Statesman*, 30 June.

Roca-Cuberes, Carles. 2013. Political interviews in public television and commercial broadcasters: A comparison. *Discourse and Communication*, 8: 155–179.

Romaniuk, Tanya. 2013. Pursuing answers to questions in broadcast journalism. *Research on Language and Social Interaction*, 46: 144–164.

Ryle, Gilbert. 1949. *The Concept of Mind*. Chicago, IL: University of Chicago Press.

Sacks, Harvey. 1963. Sociological description. *Berkeley Journal of Sociology*, 8: 1–16.

Sacks, Harvey. 1972. An initial investigation of the usability of conversational data for doing sociology. In *Studies in Social Interaction*, edited by David Sudnow, 31–74. New York, NY: Free Press.

Sacks, Harvey. 1984. Notes on methodology. In *Structures of Social Action: Studies in Conversation Analysis*, edited by J. Maxwell Atkinson and John Heritage, 21–27. Cambridge: Cambridge University Press.

Sacks, Harvey. 1987. On the preferences for agreement and contiguity in sequences in conversation. In *Talk and Social Organisation*, edited by Graham Button and John R.E. Lee, 54–69. Clevedon: Multilingual Matters.

Sacks, Harvey. 1992. *Lectures on Conversation (2 Vols.)*. Oxford: Blackwell.

Sacks, Harvey, Emanuel A. Schegloff, and Gail Jefferson. 1974. A simplest systematics for the organization of turn-taking for conversation. *Language*, 50: 696–735.

Scannell, Paddy. 1989. Public service broadcasting and modern public life. *Media, Culture and Society*, 11: 135–166.

Scannell, Paddy. 1991. Introduction: The relevance of talk. In *Broadcast Talk*, edited by Paddy Scannell, 1–13. London: Sage.

Scannell, Paddy, and David Cardiff. 1991. *A Social History of British Broadcasting (Vol. 1)*. Oxford: Blackwell.

Scheflen, Albert, and Alice Scheflen. 1972. *Body Language and the Social Order*. Englewood Cliffs, NJ: Prentice Hall.

Schegloff, Emanuel A. 1968. Sequencing in conversational openings. *American Anthropologist*, 70: 1075–1095.

Schegloff, Emanuel A. 1982. Discourse as an interactional achievement: Some uses of "uh huh" and other things that come between sentences. In *Analysing Discourse: Text and Talk*, edited by Deborah Tannen, 71–93. Washington DC: Georgetown University Press.

Schegloff, Emanuel A. 1989. From interview to confrontation: Observations on the Bush/Rather encounter. *Research on Language and Social Interaction*, 22: 215–240.

Schegloff, Emanuel A. 1988. Presequences and indirection: Applying speech act theory to ordinary conversation. *Journal of Pragmatics*, 12: 55–62.

Schegloff, Emanuel A. 2007. *Sequence Organization in Interaction*. Cambridge: Cambridge University Press.

Schegloff, Emanuel A., and Gene Lerner. 2009. Beginning to respond: *Well*-prefaced responses to wh-questions. *Research on Language and Social Interaction*, 42: 91–115.

Schegloff, Emanuel A. and Harvey Sacks. 1973. Opening up closings. *Semiotica*, 7: 289–327.

Schegloff, Emanuel A., Gail Jefferson, and Harvey Sacks. 1975. The preference for self-correction in the organization of repair in conversation. *Language*, 53: 361–382.

Schlesinger, Philip. 1978. *Putting "Reality" Together: BBC News*. London: Methuen.

Schudson, Michael. 1994. Question authority: A history of the news interview in American journalism, 1860s–1930s. *Media, Culture and Society*, 16: 565–588.

Silverman, David. 2017. How was it for you? The Interview Society and the irresistible rise of the (poorly analyzed) interview. *Qualitative Research*, 17: 144–158.

Silvia, Tony, ed. 2001. *Global News: Perspectives on the Information Age*. Ames, IA: Iowa State University Press.

Smith, Dinitia. 2001. No regrets for a love of explosives; In a memoir of sorts, a war protester talks of life with the Weathermen. *New York Times*, September 11.

Speer, Susan A., and Ian Hutchby. 2003. From ethics to analytics: Aspects of participants' orientations to the presence and relevance of recording technologies. *Sociology*, 37: 315–337.

Steensen, Steen. 2019. Journalism's epistemic crisis and its solution: Disinformation, datafication and source criticism. *Journalism*, 20: 185–189.

Sterbenz, Christina. 2014. "So here's why everyone is starting sentences with the word 'so'." *Business Insider*, May 12.
Strömbäck, Jesper. 2008. Four phases of mediatisation: An analysis of the mediatisation of politics. *International Journal of Press/Politics*, 13: 228–246.
Ten Have, Paul. 1998. *Doing Conversation Analysis*. London: Sage.
Terasaki, Alene. 2004. Pre-announcement sequences in conversation. In *Conversation Analysis: Studies from the First Generation*, edited by Gene Lerner, 171–224. Amsterdam: John Benjamins.
Thompson, John. 1984. *Studies in the Theory of Ideology*. Cambridge: Polity Press.
Thompson, John. 2000. *Political Scandal: Power and Visibility in the Media Age*. Cambridge: Polity Press.
Thornborrow, Joanna. 2010. "Going public": Constructing the personal in a television news interview. *Discourse and Communication*, 4: 105–124.
Thornborrow, Joanna. 2014. *The Discourse of Public Participation Media: From Talk Show to Twitter*. London: Routledge.
Thornborrow, Joanna, and Martin Montgomery, eds. 2010. Special Issue: *Personalisation in the Broadcast News Interview*. *Discourse and Communication*, 4: 99–219.
Thussu, Daya Kishan. 2008. *News as Entertainment: The Rise of Global Infotainment*. London: Sage.
Tolson, Andrew, ed. 2001. *Television Talk Shows: Discourse, Performance, Spectacle*. Mahwah, NJ: Lawrence Erlbaum Associates.
Tolson, Andrew. 2006. *Media Talk: Spoken Discourse on TV and Radio*. Edinburgh: Edinburgh University Press.
Tuchman, Gaye. 1978. *Making News: A Study in the Construction of Reality*. New York, NY: Free Press.
Waterson, Jim. 2019. The political interview is not dead—but it is on life support. *The Guardian*, 23 August.
Weidner, Matylda. 2016. The particle *no* in Polish talk-in-interaction. In *Nu/Na: A Family of Discourse Markers across Europe and Beyond*, edited by Peter Auer and Yael Maschler, 104–131. Berlin: de Gruyter.
Wittgenstein, Ludwig. 1953. *Philosophical Investigations*. Oxford: Oxford University Press.
Zelizer, Barbie. 2019. Resetting journalism in the aftermath of Brexit and Trump. *European Journal of Communication*, 33: 140–156.

Index

Accountability interview, 11, 71, 88, 95, 107, 116-117, 121, 127, 142, 159, 165–168
Action-opposition sequence, 117
Adjacency pairs, 23-25
Adversarial political interview, 14 78–79, 88, 116, 141 160, 168
Arenas of language use, 2, 17, 141
Arminen, I., 20
Atkinson, J. M., 20, 25, 28, 73
Atkinson, P., 3, 6, 50
Austin, J.L., 22
Authenticity, 3–6, 12, 50

Bateson, G., 22
Baym, G., 12
Bell, A., 8
Benckler, Y., 163
Bigotgate, 38
Birdwhistell, R., 22
Blumer, H., 3
Boden, D., 20
Bogen, D., 74
Bolden, G., 100
Boukes, M., 12
Brants, K., 12
Brexit, 102, 103, 163, 164
Brooker, C., 47
Bull, P., 26, 31, 36, 76

Cable news, 7, 12, 115, 148
Carbaugh, D., 4
Chadwick, A., 8, 9, 13, 32, 37, 160
Chomsky, N., 21
Clark, H. H., 17
Clayman, S., 2, 3, 5, 6, 9, 10, 12, 13, 25, 26, 31, 32, 44, 60, 61, 74, 77, 78, 80, 81, 88, 113, 116, 131, 140, 141, 159, 160, 165, 167
Coesemans, R., 9, 12, 115
Coleman, S., 6
Collins, J., 164
Cone, J., 147
Conlan, T., 4
Conversation analysis, 10, 13, 17, 159, 167
  origins of, 18–20
  methodology, 20–25
  applications of, 25–29
Conventional political interview, 13, 14, 15, 51, 140, 149, 151
Corner, J., 50, 140
Coulter, J., 14, 115

D'Ancona, M., 137, 162
Davis, E., 137, 162
Depperman, A., 100
Drew, P., 20, 25, 28, 73

Index

Ekström, M., 3, 9, 11, 12, 13, 31, 34, 47, 48, 115
Elliott, P., 2
Emotional heightening, 14, 122, 127, 130–131, 151
Epistemic authority, 79, 101, 102, 104, 114
Epistemic crisis, 163, 164, 166
Eriksson, G., 31
Emmertsen, S., 10
Evasiveness, 24, 74, 49, 80, 89, 95, 97, 122, 165

Fairclough, N., 7, 13, 27, 99
Faris, R., 163
Footing shifts, 60-64, 73, 142, 149, 150, 153
Formulations, 65–70, 98, 109, 110, 111, 121
Fowler, R., 167
Frankel, R., 29

Gaffes, 32
   media configuration of, 33, 34, 35–48
   and journalistic ethics, 49–50
Gans, H., 167
Garcia, A., 117
Garfinkel, H., 19, 21, 27
Garton, G., 36
Glogger, I., 12
Goffman, E., 19, 60, 61, 99
Golding, P., 2
Goodwin, M. H., 134, 139
Greatbatch, D., 10, 13, 25, 26, 84, 97, 117, 152
Green, D., 48

Harris, S., 26, 80, 82, 84, 121, 152
Haslett, A., 162
Hayashi, M., 100
Heaney, S., 99
Heritage, J., 2, 3, 5, 9, 10, 12, 13, 20, 25, 28, 29, 60, 65, 68, 70, 81, 88, 100, 101, 113, 114, 116, 131, 141, 160, 165, 167

Hutchby, I., 3, 10, 12, 14, 23, 25, 28, 115, 116, 117, 133, 134, 137
Hybrid media system, 2, 5, 32, 160, 161
Hybrid political interviews, 14, 15, 115
   characteristics of, 117–122
   and argument, 127–131
   and personaliztion, 135–139
   see also Emotional heightening

Interview society, 2–6, 50

James, O., 99
Jefferson, G., 19, 20, 13, 78, 93, 95, 132, 169

Kantara, A., 11, 115
Keevalik, L., 100
Kendon, A., 22
Kroon-Lundell, A., 48

Lauerbach, G., 12, 115, 140
Lerner, G., 20, 101
Levinson, S., 24
Lewis, M., 98
Loeb, L., 12, 80
Luginbühl, M., 12
Lynch, M., 74

Mast, J., 9, 12, 115
Matheson, D., 81
Maynard, D., 25, 29, 117, 134
McHoul, A., 25
Meehan, E., 9
Mediatization, *see* Total mediatization
Montgomery, M., 2, 3, 9, 11, 13, 14, 19, 36, 116, 117, 127, 140, 142, 165

Negative pre-positioning, 76, 90, 92, 108, 152
Neijens, P., 12
Nofsinger, R., 74
Non-neutrality, 115, 130, 131, 140, 154
Normative American, 150–153
Nunberg, G., 99

Otto, L., 12

Patrona, M., 3, 9, 11, 13, 115
Personalization
  see Hybrid political interview
Polar questions, 79, 80–84, 87, 88,
  109–111, 155
Pomerantz, A., 25, 74, 76, 101, 104,
  108, 139, 151
Porter, A., 38
Post-response pursuit of response,
  93–94
Post-truth, 1, 15, 157, 162, 164, 166,
  167
Prince, R., 38
Pursuit of questions
  see Polar questions

Quotativity, 88, 89, 92

Rabin-Havt, A., 137, 162
Remnick, D., 148
Rendle-Short, J., 10
Roberts, H., 163
Roca-Cuberes, C., 10
Romaniuk, T., 10, 78, 81
Ryle, G., 3

Sacks, H., 19, 20, 21, 22, 23, 24, 25, 77
Scannell, P., 7, 13, 35
Schegloff, E. A., 18, 19, 20, 21, 23, 59,
  74, 77, 101
Schlesinger, P., 2, 167
Schudson, M., 3, 7, 8, 13, 14

Silverman, D., 3, 4, 6
Silvia, T., 9
Smith, D., 148
Speech exchange systems, 18, 19, 20,
  22, 73, 115, 116, 117, 129, 130
Speer, S., 23
Steensen, S., 163
Sterbenz, C., 99
Strömbäck, J., 8

Temmerman, M., 9, 12, 115
Ten Have, P., 23
Thompson, J., 28, 34
Thornborrow, J., 3, 4, 9, 11, 42, 140
Thussu, D. K., 9, 12
Tolson, A., 3, 4, 11, 36, 115
Total mediatization, 6–8, 15, 31, 33, 42,
  49, 50
Tribuneship, 1, 15, 141, 159
  general, 142
  tendentious, 143–146, 149–153
  contested, 154–157
Tuchman, G., 167
Turn-initial particles, 100–101
Types of political interview, 12–14

Watergate, 5
Waterson, J., 161, 164
Weidner, M., 100
Wittgenstein, L., 22

Zelizer, B., 162, 163, 166
Zimmerman, D., 10, 20

About the Author

Ian Hutchby is honorary Professor of Sociology at the University of York, England. He previously held Chairs in Sociology at the University of Leicester, England, and at Brunel University, London, England. For more than thirty years Hutchby's research has contributed to the field of conversation analysis, especially in the areas of broadcast talk and political communication, interaction and technology, children's talk and the discourse of psychotherapy. He is the author of more than sixty articles and ten books, including *Confrontation Talk: Arguments, Asymmetries and Power on Talk Radio* (Lawrence Erlbaum Associates 1996), *Conversation Analysis* (with R. Wooffitt, Polity Press 1998 and 2008) and *Media Talk: Conversation Analysis and the Study of Broadcasting* (Open University Press 2006).

www.ingramcontent.com/pod-product-compliance
Lightning Source LLC
Chambersburg PA
CBHW020121010526
44115CB00008B/928